THE BREATH OF CHRIST

The Breath of Christ

Discovering the Power of the Jesus Prayer

Hoa Trung Dinh, SJ

Paulist Press
New York / Mahwah, NJ

Scripture quotations are from the New Revised Standard Version Bible: Catholic Edition, copyright © 1989, 1993 National Council of the Churches of Christ in the United States of America. Used by permission. All rights reserved worldwide.

Cover image by Black Salmon / Shutterstock.com
Cover and book design by Lynn Else

Copyright © 2025 by Hoa Trung Dinh, SJ

All rights reserved. No part of this publication may be reproduced, stored in a retrieval system, or transmitted in any form or by any means, electronic, mechanical, photocopying, recording, scanning, or otherwise, without either the prior written permission of the Publisher, or authorization through payment of the appropriate per-copy fee to the Copyright Clearance Center, Inc., www.copyright.com. Requests to the Publisher for permission should be addressed to the Permissions Department, Paulist Press, permissions@paulistpress.com.

Library of Congress Cataloging-in-Publication Data
Names: Dinh, Hoa Trung, author.
Title: The breath of Christ: discovering the power of the Jesus prayer / Hoa Trung Dinh, SJ.
Description: Paperback. | New York: Paulist Press, [2025] | Summary: "Using the Jesus Prayer, this book aims to address the pressing need to make Christian spiritual practices more accessible to ordinary Christians in their busy lives today"—Provided by publisher.
Identifiers: LCCN 2024051598 (print) | LCCN 2024051599 (ebook) | ISBN 9780809157570 (paperback) | ISBN 9780809189243 (ebook)
Subjects: LCSH: Jesus prayer.
Classification: LCC BT590.J28 D56 2025 (print) | LCC BT590.J28 (ebook) | DDC 242/.72—dc23/eng/20250324
LC record available at https://lccn.loc.gov/2024051598
LC ebook record available at https://lccn.loc.gov/2024051599

ISBN 978-0-8091-5757-0 (paperback)
ISBN 978-0-8091-8924-3 (ebook)

Published by Paulist Press
997 Macarthur Boulevard
Mahwah, New Jersey 07430
www.paulistpress.com

Printed and bound in the
United States of America

Contents

Preface ix

Introduction xi
   Daily Practice of the Jesus Prayer xiv
   The Fruits of the Jesus Prayer xvi

Chapter 1: The Jesus Prayer: History and Form 1
   From the Desert to Twenty-First-Century Christians 1
   The Right Attitude and Intention 3
   The Jesus Prayer and Hesychasm 6
   Praying the Jesus Prayer 9
   Spoken Forms of the Jesus Prayer 11

Chapter 2: Prayer as Surrender to God 14
   Inner World and Outer World 14
   Human Nature: Good or Evil? 16
   Inner Resistance to the Jesus Prayer 18
   A Diversity of Spiritual Benefits and Experiences 21
   Which Prayer Formula Should I Use? 25

Chapter 3: Turning Our Feeling into Prayer 27
   Name Our Feelings 27
   Asking for Nothing Else 31
   Braving the Inner World 33
   Self-Knowledge, Companion, Light of Consciousness 34

CONTENTS

The Breath of Christ: A Personal Journey 36
The Boundless Depths of the Jesus Prayer 38

Chapter 4: Unloading Our Burdens: Turning Anxiety
  into Prayer 41
  Recognizing Anxiety.. 42
  Anxiety: The Mind's Future Projection............................. 46
  Anxiety and the Habit Loop 50
  Observing the Anxious Thoughts: Mindfulness Meditation ... 51
  Turning Anxiety and Worries into Prayer......................... 52
  Recognizing Anxiety through the Examen 53

Chapter 5: Healing Our Psychological Traumas 55
  Understanding Psychological Trauma.............................. 56
  Healing of Past Traumas 61
  Dissolving Past Hurt through Awareness 62
  Dissolving the Pain Body: Turning Our Pain into Prayer...... 65
  A Framework for Healing of Past Traumas....................... 69

Chapter 6: Turning Anger into Prayer 72
  Understanding Anger 72
  The High Costs of Anger 73
  Ventilation Does Not Reduce Anger................................. 74
  Venting Anger on the Innocent.. 75
  The Two-Step Model: The Fuel of Anger and
    What Ignites It 77
  Principles of Anger Management 78
  Taking Time Out 79
  Reduce Stress, Reduce Anger... 80
  Turning Anger into Prayer 81

Contents

Chapter 7: Counteracting Negative Self-Talk 85
    The Inner Critic and Negative Self-Talk 86
    The Origin and Function of the Critic 87
    Is the Inner Critic the Bad Spirit? 89
    The Critic's Tactics: Cognitive Distortions 91
    How to Catch the Inner Critic 93
    How to Disarm the Inner Critic 96
    Telling Jesus about the Inner Critic 97

Chapter 8: Resistance and Surrender 99
    Surrender as the Key to Peace 100
    Surrender and Alcohol Addiction 101
    Surrender and Imminent Death 103
    Surrender and Domestic Violence 104
    Surrender and Positive Action 105
    Resistance and Suffering 106
    God's Boundless Treasures 107
    Surrender and the Jesus Prayer 109

Chapter 9: Letting Go of Our Ego 111
    Ego: The Mind-Generated Self 111
    Three Categories of Egoistic Behaviors 113
    Breaking Free from Egoistic Bondage 117

Coming Home 119

Notes 121

Preface

Life is difficult, and none of us can do it alone.

We long for meaningful relationships but are discouraged by past hurts and disappointments. We may have many friends and followers on social media but still feel lonely and empty inside. We get stuck in feelings of anger or guilt about our past and endless worries about the future.

The good news is that we don't have to face these challenges alone. We can heal from past hurt and let go of worries about the future. A loyal and trustworthy friend can support us through life's ups and downs and give us comfort and strength to overcome any difficulties.

This book is written from the perspective of someone who has faced these challenges and found a faithful friend to support them through it all—the living Christ. The Jesus Prayer is a way to connect with him. However, the idea of prayer can be daunting for many Christians, especially in the midst of life's chaos and emotional turmoil.

This book offers a transformative approach to prayer. Drawing on insights from psychology, neuroscience, and spiritual wisdom, it uncovers a pathway that engages our present experiences and turns them into prayer. This practice helps quiet the mind, release past burdens, and find refuge in the Divine. The Jesus Prayer is not a mechanical repetition of words but a sacred invitation to bring Christ's saving presence into your inner reality. It is a prayer of intimacy and surrender, offering connection and support amid life's challenges. Whether you are struggling with anxiety, anger, past trauma, or self-criticism, *The Breath of Christ* provides a pathway to healing through the transformative power of the Jesus Prayer. This prayer invites us to deeply breathe in the Divine love that surrounds us and anchor our souls in the truth of God's presence.

This book was made possible thanks to the support and encouragement of my family, colleagues, friends, and companions, especially my Jesuit brethren. I am deeply grateful to the Faber House Jesuit Community in Melbourne and the Sacred Heart Novitiate Jesuit Community in Manila for their support. I also thank the Vietnamese Christian Life Communities in Worcester, Massachusetts; Philadelphia, Pennsylvania; and Fairfax, Virginia, the prayer group Tâm Tình Giêsu in Melbourne, and members of the Vietnamese Catholic Marriage and Family Enrichment Program in Melbourne and Sydney, who have practiced this prayer method and shared its fruits with me.

I extend my gratitude to Fr. Kevin Lenehan, Dr. Catherine Playoust, and the staff of the Catholic Theological College for their invaluable support, including the research grant they provided during my study leave in early 2022. I also thank Fr. Wrex Woolnough, St. Ignatius Parish Toowong, Sr. Kathleen Muirhead, RSCJ, and members of the Faber Retreat Centre, Brisbane, for their support during my stay at the Manresa Residence while writing this book. I am also grateful to John Gill for his guidance and Susanne Nelles for proofreading the early drafts of this book.

Finally, I dedicate this book to all who have and will join me in this prayer. You are all part of this communion through the Jesus Prayer.

As the Risen Christ breathed on his disciples to endow them with the Holy Spirit, may his sacred breath guide your journey, awaken in you a renewed sense of faith, deepen your self-awareness, and connect you more deeply with the source of all life.

Introduction

In the summer of 2010, I was delighted to discover again the little book titled *The Way of a Pilgrim*, a nineteenth-century Russian work by an unknown author. The first time I read this work was during my novitiate in Australia. This little book left a deep impression on my mind. That summer, I found a Vietnamese translation of the work with the title *Người Lữ Hành Nga* (based on the French translation *Le Pélerin Russe*), published in Vietnam in 2008. Again, it filled me with joy as I read it.

The book begins like this: "By the grace of God I am a Christian man, by my actions a great sinner, and by calling a homeless wanderer of the humblest birth who roams from place to place. My worldly goods are a knapsack with some dried bread in it on my back, and in my breast pocket a Bible. And that is all."[1] It all began one Sunday when he went to church to pray. As he heard a passage being read from the First Epistle of St. Paul to the Thessalonians, three words resonated in him, "Pray without ceasing" (1 Thess 5:17). This text became a puzzle for him, an urgent, demanding problem that would not go away. How is it possible to pray without ceasing? Sure, we can devote some periods to prayer each day, but after that, we must attend to our daily activities. How can one commit the time and energy to pray without ceasing? Still, he thought, it must be possible; otherwise, the Apostle would not have urged us to do so.

Thus, the pilgrim sets out on his way. He visits churches to hear famous preachers, hoping that they might shed some light on the problem. He attends many fine sermons on prayer—what it is, how much we need it, and what its fruits are. But none tells him how he can pray without ceasing.

THE BREATH OF CHRIST

Finally, he comes on a starets (a spiritual guide) who shows him the way. The prayer that doesn't stop, according to the starets, is the Jesus Prayer: the continual calling upon the name of Jesus with the lips, in the spirit, with the breathing, and in the heart, while imploring his grace during every occupation—at all times, in all places, even during sleep. The prayer is simply this: "Lord Jesus Christ, have mercy on me." The prayer consists of the holy name of Jesus and a short petition prayer. Once you are accustomed to this prayer, you will experience so profound a consolation and so great a need to recite it that you can no longer live without it. And it will begin to voice itself within you of its own accord.

A little note on prayer. Prayer can be correctly defined as establishing an interior connection with God. From my own experience, prayer is even better defined as an interior act of open surrender to God. It is the admission of one's total defeat and surrender: "OK God, you win!" "I can't do it on my own!" It is the honest admission that I am not God. "I can't save myself, Lord! And I am done resisting you!" Prayer is opening the gateway for God, just as an army general, having fought long and fierce battles defending his castle, at last, admits defeat and lets down the drawbridge. Prayer is to lay down one's arms and surrender, "You can come in now, and we will talk!" Prayer is that openness, that total surrender of oneself to God's love. That is precisely when transformation occurs when we experience forgiveness and love. That is when we are healed of our hurts and fears, lifted into friendship with Jesus and communion with God's holy people.

That is prayer. But how do we pray? We need a practice to cultivate a habit of prayer that fosters the interior act of surrender to God in our hearts and will. The Jesus Prayer is a very efficacious spiritual practice that goes back to the monastic desert fathers in the fifth century. Regrettably, this spiritual practice has little place in our contemporary life, and yet many energetic Christians turn

Introduction

to Zen meditation or Yoga practice in their search for spiritual nourishment. The Jesus Prayer is an effective Christian practice that can nourish the soul and foster spiritual growth amid the constant demands of our modern life.

Back to the pilgrim. For the first two days, the pilgrim is instructed to repeat the prayer three thousand times each day. Then six thousand times a day for the next two days. He is then told to repeat it twelve thousand times a day, and then without limits. Then what happens? The first two days are difficult. After that, the prayer "became so easy and likeable, that as soon as I stopped, I felt a sort of need to go on saying [it]....I grew so used to my prayer that when I stopped for a single moment I felt...as though something was missing, as though I had lost something. The very moment I started the prayer again, it went on easily and joyously."[2]

The prayer then begins to wake him up in the morning. Then it is as if his lips and tongue pronounce the words by themselves, without any effort. He comes to feel light as if he were walking on air. And his world is transformed. "I felt there was no happier person on earth than I, and I doubted if there could be greater and fuller happiness in the kingdom of heaven....The whole outside world also seemed to me full of charm and delight. Everything drew me to love and thank God: people, trees, plants, and animals. I saw them all as my kinfolk; I found on all of them the magic of the name of Jesus."[3]

I have practiced this prayer for the last thirteen years. I find it a most effective and fulfilling form of prayer. It has a mysterious power that helps remove all the obstacles to inner peace and abundant life. It helps settle the messiness of daily life by turning everything into prayer. I use a simple Vietnamese phrase, *Giêsu, xin cứu giúp con!* (Lord Jesus, help me!). When I started, I found it extremely hard to recite the prayer. At first, I tried to link it with the rhythm of my breathing: on breathing in, I prayed "Lord Jesus," asking the Lord to come and fill my lungs, my body, mind, and soul; on breathing out, I prayed "help me!" breathing out the anxiety, pressures, fears, and pains within me. In the early days, I could repeat the prayer only once or twice before being fed up and distracted. Such a simple task and utterly impossible to do! Then I realized one day that I struggled so much to do the prayer, not because it was useless but because I had an internal resistance to it. There were powerful forces within me that fought against the prayer. Deep down, I did not want Jesus to come into my heart because I feared he would change everything and take away my freedom. Somewhere in my psyche, I did not want God's kingdom to come for fear that God would abolish my kingdom and destroy my castles and shrines. In my heart, I still wanted to be the lord of my kingdom. It was the Jesus Prayer that shed light on my inner reality. I did not have the interior freedom to open myself to God, nor did I trust Jesus as much as I had thought.

Therefore, practicing the Jesus Prayer is the key to surrendering to God. It is a tremendous act of faith to surrender each day to find myself in God. It is to entreat "Your kingdom come!" despite my resistance. When the practitioner comes to a total surrender to God, letting go of their objectives and agenda, they will experience a deep sense of peace, lightness, and joy within. They will find endless peace and joy in their soul each day, where God resides if they have the courage to surrender themselves.

Amen. Lord, come and rule in our hearts. Lord Jesus, help me!

DAILY PRACTICE OF THE JESUS PRAYER

Each day, I spend ten minutes in the morning offering the day to God and ten minutes at night reviewing the day before sleep.

Each morning, I pray by inviting Jesus into everything I do. I

Introduction

begin with a sign of reverence toward God: like making the Sign of the Cross or bowing reverently to God.

Then I name everything on my mind or what I plan for today, inviting Jesus to be part of my day. For instance,

* *Lord, today I have to go to work, but I feel a little tired. Lord Jesus, help me!*
* *Lord, today I have an appointment. I feel anxious because I am unsure how it will turn out. Lord Jesus, help me!*
* *Lord, my daughter was coughing after school yesterday. I am so worried that it might be COVID-19. Lord Jesus, help me!*
* *Lord, they have laid off many people at work. I've been anxious about my job. Lord Jesus, help me!*
* *Today I will see that grumpy person at work again! Lord Jesus, help me!*

I tell Jesus everything that comes to my mind without holding back. Every cause for anxiety, everything I'm looking forward to with delight, every worry and fear, every plan and intent—I share it all with Jesus and ask for his assistance. I finish this ten minutes with an Our Father.

In the evening, I spend another ten minutes with Jesus. I begin again with a sign of reverence. I then look back on everything that occurred during the day and empty my heart to the Lord.

* *Lord, today I came out of work feeling very stressed, hungry, and tired. Lord Jesus, help me!*
* *Lord, today that person upset me. Lord Jesus, help me!*
* *Lord, I didn't finish the work I was supposed to do today. I am a little anxious. Lord Jesus, help me!*
* *Lord, I shouted at my son today. I feel so bad! Lord Jesus, help me!*
* *Lord, I am pleased that I visited my mum today. Lord Jesus, help me!*

THE BREATH OF CHRIST

* *Lord, tomorrow I have to do something quite difficult; I hope it will turn out well. Lord Jesus, help me!*
* *Lord, I don't know how to pray correctly. Lord Jesus, help me!*

In love and trust, I share with Jesus everything that troubles or burdens me and everything I am grateful for or enjoy during the day. I finish with an Our Father.

If we pray intentionally and with sincerity, we will immediately experience lightness within because Jesus is never far from those who call upon him. Jesus will come to us and provide assistance and guidance.

In the beginning, we often find it difficult, uncomfortable, awkward....Why must I disclose my stuff? Nevertheless, once we overcome the temptation to give up, we will reach the authentic prayer in our hearts, and our lives will be transformed. We will find peace and deep joy; our hearts will no longer be heavy, anxious, fearful, or upset.

Life is hard. We need God's assistance in everything we do. The prayer opens us up to receive Jesus's presence in every situation and moment of our life. Through this prayer, Jesus becomes our companion in everything that we do.

The heart that knows how to pray will never be lonely. God will become our life and our hope if we have the courage to surrender to him.

* *Lord, teach us to pray. Lord Jesus, help me!*

THE FRUITS OF THE JESUS PRAYER

Unloading My Burdens: I share with Jesus all the burdens of worries I am carrying.

Introduction

- *Lord, I am exhausted! I feel so overburdened and tired! Lord Jesus, help me!*
- *I have something to do, but I get worried and stressed whenever I think of it. Lord Jesus, help me!*

Emptying My Rubbish: I give to Jesus all the rubbish I carry inside: anger, frustration, upset, disappointment, discontent.

- *Lord, how dare he say that to me? I am so angry! Lord Jesus, help me!*

Healing My Wounds and Dissolving My Pain Body: The prayer helps heal psychological traumas, leading to forgiveness, reconciliation, freedom, and peace.

- *Lord, whenever I think of that incident, I feel upset, hurt, and angry. Lord Jesus, help me!*

Counteracting Negative Self-Talk: In times of crisis, vulnerability, or stress, the negative self-talk becomes activated in me. The prayer helps me overcome the paralyzing sense of guilt, shame, and self-punishment.

- *Lord, I am judging myself and beating myself up again. Lord Jesus, help me!*

Deflating My Bubble: When someone points out my fault, I often inflate the bubble to protect my ego. I am tempted to deny, criticize, or blame someone else. The prayer helps deflate my bubble: acknowledge my fault and amend it to grow closer to God and others.

- *Lord, when that person said I was at fault, I was so angry and wanted to get back at them. Lord Jesus, help me!*

THE BREATH OF CHRIST

Surrender Prayer: When something undesirable happens, I tend to react negatively by resisting, complaining, or blaming, which leads to a loss of inner peace. The prayer helps me accept the choices available to me in each life situation, no matter how limited, and let go of my resistance to things about which I have no choice. Once I surrender, I respond to each life situation with awareness and intentionality instead of reacting negatively.

* *Lord, I have lost my job! This is terrible because I have to earn money to support my family. Lord Jesus, help me!*

Protecting My Space: When I feel under enemy attack, troubled with doubt, confusion, or overwhelmed by fear, I keep watch and pray for protection.

* *Lord, I am overwhelmed with these temptations and feel so weak. Lord Jesus, help me!*

Coming Home: When I feel fed up, lonely, isolated, or unloved, the prayer takes me home to my Father's house, where I am loved, cherished, forgiven, and healed. I find peace and rest in God.

* *Lord, I feel so lonely. Lord Jesus, help me!*
* *Lord, I feel so bored and so fed up. Lord Jesus, help me!*

Accompanying people from diverse cultures and languages, I have found reciting the Jesus Prayer in our native tongue most effective because it gives us a sense of coming home where we are safe and free to be ourselves.

Filipino (Tagalog):

Panginoon Hesus, tulungan mo ako! (Lord Jesus, help me!)
Hesus, tulungan mo ako! (Jesus, help me!)

Introduction

Bisaya (Cebuano):

Hesus, tabangi ako. (Jesus, help me!)

English:

Lord Jesus, help me!
Lord Jesus, save me!
Come, Lord Jesus!
Lord Jesus, have mercy on me!

Chinese:

主耶稣，请帮助我！ *(Zhǔ Yēsū, qǐng bāngzhù wǒ!)*
  (Lord Jesus, help me!)
耶稣，请帮助我！ *(Yēsū, qǐng bāngzhù wǒ!)*
  (Jesus, help me!)

Japanese:

主イエスよ、助けてください！
  (Shu Iesuyo, tasuketekudasai!) (Lord Jesus, help me!)
主イエスよ、救ってください！
  (Shu Iesuyo, sukutte kudasai!) (Lord Jesus, save me!)

Spanish:

Jesus, ten compasión de mi! (Jesus, have mercy on me!)

Vietnamese:

Giêsu, xin cứu giúp con! (Iesu sin kúu yúp kon)
  (Jesus, help me!)

1

The Jesus Prayer
History and Form

Gemma is a widowed mother of three who works hard to maintain a small business in the clothing industry to support her family. She writes: "I pray the Jesus Prayer in the morning, evening, and throughout the day, especially when things get difficult. I often say this prayer, 'Lord, I am anxious when I find my child unwell. Lord Jesus, help me!' I feel an easing of anxiety each time I speak to the Lord. It strengthens my faith and assures me that the Lord always loves me, accompanies me, and supports me. When I repeat this prayer over and over, I gradually gain insights into my conduct toward my children and what I should do to support them."

FROM THE DESERT TO TWENTY-FIRST-CENTURY CHRISTIANS

The Jesus Prayer originates in the spiritual practices of the desert ascetics of Egypt in the fourth century. In response to St. Paul's injunction "Pray without ceasing" (1 Thess 5:17), the monks and nuns developed a prayer practice that continually repeated a single word or phrase as they engaged in daily manual tasks. This prayer discipline, known as "monologic prayer" (or *monologia*),

THE BREATH OF CHRIST

helps practitioners always remember God as they go about their daily lives. This spiritual practice of repetition also helps free the mind from distractions.[1]

The phrases used by the ascetics of Egypt for monologic prayer were most often taken from Scripture, especially the Book of Psalms. For example: "*Have mercy on me, O God, according to Your great mercy*" (Ps. 50 [51]:1); "*O God, come to my aid; O Lord, make haste to help me*" (Ps. 69 [70]:1). There were also prayer formulae that contained the name of Jesus: "*Jesus, help me*"; "*Lord Jesus, protect me from my tongue.*"[2] These are the earliest forms of the Jesus Prayer, though they enjoyed no special recognition among various forms of monologic prayer in the fourth century. Into the fifth century, the Jesus Prayer came to have an important place in the emerging Jesus-centered spirituality.

St. Diadochos, who was a bishop of Photiki in northern Greece during the mid-fifth century, played a significant role in the evolution of the Jesus Prayer. He emphasized the significance of constantly remembering and invoking the Lord's name during prayer. He proposed that by continuously invoking the Lord's name, one can calm the mind.

> When we have blocked all its outlets by means of the remembrance of God, the intellect requires of us imperatively some task which will satisfy its need for activity. We should give it nothing but the prayer "Lord Jesus" to complete its purpose. "No one," it is written, "can say 'Lord Jesus' except in the Holy Spirit" (1 Cor. 12:3). Let the intellect continually concentrate on these words within its inner shrine with such intensity that it is not turned aside to any mental images.[3]

This early author alludes to the fruits of invoking the holy name: stillness of the mind, purification of the soul, sharpening of perception, and a greater love for the Lord.[4]

The earliest text to cite the Jesus Prayer in its fully developed form is *A Discourse on Abba Philimon*, written perhaps between the sixth and seventh centuries.[5] When asked how to overcome distractions, Abba Philimon suggested the inward meditation and explained it in this way: "Keep watch in your heart; and with watchfulness say in your mind with awe and trembling: 'Lord Jesus Christ, have mercy upon me.'"[6]

The standard formula, "Lord Jesus Christ, Son of God, have mercy on me," was developed over several centuries of Christian spiritual practice. As the eminent modern-day teacher of the prayer Metropolitan Kallistos Ware points out, this formula contains four essential elements in Christian spirituality. First, it is *the cry for mercy*. *Kyrie eleison*, "Lord have mercy," is grounded in Scripture and found in Christian liturgy from ancient times. Mercy signifies the healing love of God pouring out on those who call upon him. Second, the *discipline of repetition* or monologic prayer helps practitioners remember God always. Third, it is the *quest for stillness* (*hesychia*). In the words of Evagrius Ponticus (346–399), "When you are praying, do not shape within yourself any image of the Deity, and do not let your intellect be stamped with the impress of any form;…For prayer means the shedding of thoughts."[7] Instead of calling to mind an image or a gospel story of Jesus, we dwell in his immediate presence in the now.[8] In this regard, the Jesus Prayer differs from the methods of discursive meditation found in *lectio divina* in Western Christianity or the Spiritual Exercises of St. Ignatius of Loyola. Fourth, it is the *veneration of the holy name*. Invoking the Lord's name opens a gateway for a personal encounter with the living Christ.[9]

THE RIGHT ATTITUDE AND INTENTION

The spiritual masters of Eastern Christianity insist that the prayer must be said with concentration, compunction, and faith.[10] It is not to be recited mechanically or used simply as an impersonal mantra, for it is an invocation addressed in faith to the living Lord. The mind is to focus on the personal presence of Jesus but not engage in any mental images or discursive thoughts. Practitioners ought to amend their lives and cultivate the appropriate attitude for prayer. Keeping the commandments, asceticism, humility, and repentance for sin are emphasized. In today's context, ideally, the Jesus Prayer is practiced by people who are part of a Church community where they find support and guidance in the spiritual path and participation in the liturgical and sacramental life of the Church. It is helpful for a practitioner to be assisted by an experienced spiritual guide. It is not advisable to force one's spiritual progress or seek advanced levels of contemplation for which one is not ready.[11]

During a sabbatical some years ago, I had many "brilliant ideas" and a strong desire to use the Jesus Prayer to create an accessible path toward spiritual enlightenment. While listening to Thich Nhat Hanh and other spiritual masters, I felt inspired to attempt an interreligious project. The goal was to combine spiritual insights and practices from Christianity and Buddhism to create a new pathway that would reflect the richness of both traditions. Buddhist spiritual masters offer valuable insights into the human psyche, the false self with its constant cravings and resistance, and the state of enlightenment that is filled with freedom, understanding, and compassion that comes when the false self is dissolved. The Buddhist path to enlightenment is the path of mindfulness through practice and learning. However, it is a challenging path, and only a few individuals can attain enlightenment through mindfulness alone. I thought that Christianity could surely offer an easier way to enlightenment. Undoubtedly, the Jesus Prayer would be an effective means to achieve enlightenment through easy, practical steps that everyone can follow. I wondered if we could use the Jesus Prayer to achieve stillness and mindfulness. Perhaps we could use the prayer to make mindful eating easier for beginners. Perhaps we could use it to enhance awareness, and then, with a stronger light of awareness, we could dissolve the false self and attain enlightenment.

For weeks, I tried implementing this idea of using the Jesus Prayer to enhance mindfulness practices in meditation and eating. However, my attempts proved fruitless, and I could not achieve the desired results. I tried again and again but still failed. I eventually gave up after intense effort without any success. It took me six months to realize what was wrong with my idea. I learned that the Jesus Prayer should not be used as a means to attain spiritual enlightenment for personal gain. The idea of using the Lord's name as a tool to achieve my spiritual goals was based on arrogance and presumption. I realized that my strong desire for spiritual goods was driven by my ego's need to enhance itself. The Jesus Prayer cannot be used to achieve our personal desires or attain spiritual goods. When we use the Jesus Prayer in this way, we are serving the ego, which is blasphemous and in violation of the second commandment.

This experience emphasizes the importance of having the right attitude of reverence, humility, faith, and love as we pray the Jesus Prayer. This prayer serves as a gateway into a personal relationship with the living Christ, our Lord. Christ has given himself in love for our salvation and made himself accessible through the invocation of his name. We must be cautious not to become arrogant or presumptuous as we become more familiar with the Lord's name. As we walk on our spiritual journey, we face countless temptations to prioritize things over Christ. These temptations include not only worldly goods such as wealth, social status, and pleasure but also spiritual goods such as spiritual knowledge, powers, and enlightenment.

It is appropriate to set goals for ourselves and ask for the Lord's help as we work toward these goals because asking for divine assistance is the essence of this prayer. For instance, we can seek healing for our past traumas as our goal and ask the Lord for assistance and guidance as we work on our healing process. Similarly, we can seek peace of mind as our goal and ask the Lord for guidance in invoking his name. However, we must be cautious not to use the Lord's name as a magic formula to get what we want or as engine fuel to get us from point A to point B. This attitude would be presumptuous and blasphemous. On the other hand, it is entirely appropriate to approach the Lord with our needs and ask for his guidance and assistance. Put simply, using the Lord's name to get what we want is wrong and ineffective, whereas coming to the Lord with our needs and asking for his guidance and assistance is the right and effective approach.

In later chapters, we will discuss in more detail how we might come to the Lord with our specific needs and implore his help, which is radically different from using the Lord's name to attain our end.

THE JESUS PRAYER AND HESYCHASM

Within the Orthodox tradition, hesychasm is the primary spiritual practice through which the Jesus Prayer has been prayed over the centuries. Hesychasm ("quietness" in Greek) became well known as the mystical prayer of the monks of Mount Athos through the teachings of St. Gregory of Sinai in the fourteenth century. According to St. Gregory, prayer is the action of God within us.[12] It activates the grace we receive at baptism. Prayer practice aims to bring to life the divine presence within us and remove the obstacles of sin so that the grace of baptism may become realized as a lived experience. As Gregory explains, the energy of the Holy Spirit we receive at baptism is realized more rapidly through the continuous invocation of the Lord Jesus with mindfulness of God.[13]

Gregory provides instructions on the physical and inner aspects of hesychasm. The hesychast is to keep the mind in the heart and recite "Lord Jesus Christ, have mercy on me" while practicing breathing control to still the mind.[14] The hesychast is to perse-

The Jesus Prayer

vere diligently with ardent longing, seeking the Lord in their heart despite physical pain or mental discomfort. The physical technique is used to help the mind concentrate, but it is not an essential element of the Jesus Prayer.

Inwardly, Gregory insists that the invocation be as continuous as possible and kept free from all mental images. The Jesus Prayer should be recited continually, sometimes with the lips, at other times by the mind alone so the practitioner can come to stillness and unity. He stresses that the mind is kept free from colors, images, and forms. The hesychast is to lay aside thoughts, imagination, and *phantasia*. As we have seen above in Diodochus, the remembrance of God can reduce the outlets of the mind and bring it to stillness.

A significant aspect of hesychastic prayer is to "contain the mind within the heart." The heart (*kardia*) here indicates not only the physical organ but the spiritual center of the person, the true self, where the mystery of one's union with God is realized.[15] As Kallistos Ware points out, the Orthodox tradition regards the heart as the center of personhood. It includes emotions, the will, reason, and the higher faculty of awareness known in Greek as the *nous*. The heart is the spiritual center of the person, the point of encounter with God, the gateway to self-transcendence, and the dwelling place of Christ. "Prayer of the heart" means prayer not just of the emotions but of the whole person, including the body and soul. If prayer is to actualize the divine presence within, "prayer of the heart" is both the human and divine activity through which Christ becomes a living presence in us. It is the living Christ who prays in me and with me during the practice of the Jesus Prayer.[16]

If the "heart" means the whole person, how can we understand the idea of *keeping the mind in the heart*?

If you practice mindfulness meditation, you will notice that the mind is a very active creature with a life of its own. Like a dog in the park, it is distracted easily and goes off in pursuit of trivial things. It constantly races into the future or dashes to the past to check things out, figure things out, or resolve things it deems problematic. Just like a dog, the mind can get attracted to certain things or become repulsed, scared, or angry by other things. Attraction, repulsion, fear, and anger are emotional responses to what the mind sees in its wanderings. A dog might run after things or bark at people or other dogs when frightened or upset. In a similar way, the mind can easily become preoccupied with pursuing attractive things, getting lost in trying to solve problems, or judging things that are upsetting or frightening.

In this state of distraction, which is normal for most of us, the mind is dispersed, and our attention is drawn away from the present moment and our body. According to Gregory's spiritual theology, this constant distraction of the mind results from the Fall. Initially simple and unitary before the Fall, the human mind now suffers division and fragmentation due to Adam's sin. Through invoking the holy name, our mind can return to its original simplicity and unity.[17] The hesychastic prayer helps quiet the mind and bring its attention back to the present moment. As the mind returns to the here and now, it becomes aware of the sounds in the outer world and the body sensations, emotions, and thoughts in the inner world. To keep "the mind in the heart" is to keep one's attention on the inner world so one can be aware of one's body sensations, emotions, thoughts, and other mental activities.

For a mindfulness practitioner, keeping one's attention on the inner world is essential to meditation. One can observe the mind in its activities by being intensely attentive to the inner world. Watching one's mind means ceasing to identify oneself with the mind and being at some distance from the mind's activities. During mindfulness practice, our attention is constantly drawn to the mind's activities, and we are lost in thoughts. What we do consciously when we become aware of this distraction is to turn our full attention to the present moment and observe our feelings and thoughts again. For most people, mindfulness meditation involves going back and forth between mindfulness (attentive observation of the mind) and distraction (being drawn into mind activities). With practice, our periods of mindfulness become longer: we can observe our mind's activities for more extended periods without being drawn into them. The hesychast uses the Jesus Prayer to help the mind return to the heart (or inner world) and to dispel distractions.

Furthermore, because our psychic energy goes wherever our attention is directed, we fuel the mind's activities with our psychic energy when we are drawn into them. When we consciously direct our attention to observing the mind's activities, we withdraw energy from them. The mind becomes quiet, like a noisy machine being unplugged from its power source. There is quietness when the mind no longer generates noisy thoughts or goes in pursuit of things. There is stillness when the heart no longer reacts to the mind's activities. There is peace, calm, tranquility, spaciousness, freedom, restfulness, and renewed vitality. These are the fruits of mindfulness meditation once we can observe our mind without reaction. However, there is much more to the fruits of hesychasm and the Jesus Prayer to which we shall return in chapter 3.

PRAYING THE JESUS PRAYER

According to Kallistos Ware, we can practice the Jesus Prayer in two ways. First, we can say it freely and as often as we can throughout the day. We can say it at the bus stop or train station, while we are driving or walking, in class or at work, in church or at home, when we are unable to sleep, feeling anxious or distressed. This continuous practice aims to find Christ everywhere. Second, we can pray during appointed times when all our attention is focused on prayer. This focused use aims to create silence.[18] Hesychasm is an example of this focused practice.

During this focused practice, sitting on a chair of suitable height is advisable to maintain a straight spine, with feet on the ground and eyes closed. The words of the prayer should be said slowly, softly, and quietly with faith and love.[19] The Jesus Prayer can also be said communally, and there are several ways this can be done. One person can lead by reciting the prayer aloud, and the others repeat it inwardly. After perhaps a hundred times, another person will take turns to recite the prayer, and so on. The community can also pray in silence, with each person saying the prayer inwardly.[20] I also have experienced a form of communal prayer in which each participant takes a turn to name their feelings, burdens, or concerns, then ends with "Lord Jesus, help me!" Then everyone repeats aloud, "Lord Jesus, help me!" This needs to occur within a smaller group where participants are asked to keep what they hear during the prayer session confidential. Each form of communal prayer can be a powerful spiritual experience for participants.

Kallistos Ware suggests that having a spiritual guide or mentor can be helpful in practicing the prayer. This guide can be either a woman or man, lay or religious, or a priest who knows the way and can assist us on our spiritual path.[21] In my own experience, practicing this prayer can bring both spiritual joy and challenges. The graces of the prayer can penetrate deep into our psyche, bringing about major changes, which can sometimes be unsettling if we do not have a guide to accompany us. It is not uncommon to face difficulties while reciting the prayer, as there are powerful inner forces that resist it. This is where an experienced spiritual guide can provide valuable assistance.

A prayer rope or rosary can help us recite the Jesus Prayer with ease and greater focus. It helps us to concentrate by involving our hands and fingers in the prayer activity. The practice of moving each knot or bead through our fingers helps steady our minds and establishes a rhythm in our prayer.[22] With practice over time, the recitation of the prayer becomes linked with the movements of the prayer knots or rosary beads through our fingers, and our fingers become habituated to the prayer practice. Each time we move the prayer rope or rosary beads through our fingers, our whole body and spirit are engaged in prayer. It can be said that *our fingers know how to pray*.

Another psychosomatic method involves linking the Jesus Prayer with the rhythm of our breathing.[23] This technique helps to focus our attention and create silence more effectively, but it requires much practice before we feel comfortable with it. One simple way to practice this technique is to recite "Lord Jesus" as we inhale and "help me" as we exhale. This technique is challenging for beginners, but once mastered, it can bring a profound sense of calm and connection to the divine presence. It is truly the experience of breathing *the breath of Christ* where one feels the fruits of coming home, such as spaciousness, joy, restfulness, inner peace, and renewed vitality.

This technique is challenging because, for many people, becoming aware of their breathing would trigger anxiety and the urge to control it. Once we try to control our breathing, we invariably feel out of breath and lose concentration. That is why before we can link the Jesus Prayer with our breathing, we need to practice awareness of breathing without controlling it. This method is to be used only so far as it is helpful. Note also that when you pray "Lord Jesus" as you breathe in, do not will to breathe Jesus into your body. Instead, feel your breath coming in and out of your body with Jesus as your co-breather, who is closer to you than you are to yourself.

SPOKEN FORMS OF THE JESUS PRAYER

The following are the most common forms in the Orthodox tradition:

* *Lord Jesus Christ, have mercy on me.* (Abba Philimon)
* *Lord Jesus Christ, Son of God, have mercy on me.* (St. Gregory of Sinai)

THE BREATH OF CHRIST

* *Lord Jesus Christ, Son of God, have mercy on me, a sinner.*
  (Patriarch Kallistos's Life of St. Gregory of Sinai)

The biblical roots of these can be found in the invocations to the Lord for mercy in the New Testament. It is the cry of the blind beggar Bartimaeus, "Jesus, Son of David, have mercy on me" (Luke 18:38; Mark 10:47). It resonates with the tax collector's humble petition in the temple, "God, be merciful to me, a sinner" (Luke 18:13).

St. Gregory of Sinai also suggested abbreviated forms for hesychastic practice:

* *Lord Jesus Christ, have mercy on me.*
* *Jesus, Son of God, have mercy on me.*
* *Lord Jesus, have mercy on me.*

Gregory allows some variation in the form, but the Hesychast ought not to make frequent changes from one to another.[24] Kallistos Ware also identifies in *The Book of Varsanuphius and John* these simple forms:

* *Lord Jesus Christ, save me.*
* *Master Jesus, protect me.*
* *Jesus, help me.*[25]

As Kallistos Ware points out, there is a degree of liberty and flexibility in the verbal forms of the prayer.[26] Instead of saying, "have mercy on me," we may say, "have mercy on us" or "have mercy on us and the world" to include others more explicitly in our prayer. We may also include the saints in our petition,

* *Lord Jesus Christ, at the prayers of the Mother of God, have mercy on me.*
* *Lord Jesus Christ, at the prayers of St...., have mercy on me.*

The Jesus Prayer

* *Lord Jesus Christ, through the protection of my guardian angel, have mercy on me.*

Kallistos Ware suggests that we are all at liberty to choose the form of words most suitable for us.[27] Like St. Gregory, he also warns against changing the form of words too often, because shrubs that are frequently transplanted do not put down roots.

For those who have advanced in prayer practice, the prayer formula can be abbreviated as "Lord Jesus, have mercy," "My Jesus," or even "Jesus." For Kallistos Ware, the term "Jesus Prayer" can be applied in principle to any short prayer that contains the holy name.[28]

As a general guide, the key to success is to choose one formula and persevere without changing it. The greatest difficulty as we begin in this prayer is the temptation to give up. So, once you choose a certain formula and have difficulty praying with it, do not change to another formula, but keep on praying until you become comfortable in praying it. This is because of the powerful forces in all of us working against the Jesus Prayer. We shall discuss this in more detail in the next chapter.

2

Prayer as Surrender to God

After a group retreat on the Jesus Prayer, Lana, a prayer companion, wrote, "I have never been to a retreat that felt as light and peaceful as this one. The participants quickly experienced the love and closeness of God through the power of the Jesus Prayer. It's amazing to see how this prayer can create beautiful melodies in people's souls when the Lord comes to their aid. Even more incredible is that if one feels resistance to the Jesus Prayer, the solution is simply to continue praying it until the resistance fades away. This truly is a remedy from heaven. I am grateful for this simplest form of prayer, but it is also the hardest because one has to persevere without ceasing. The shortest path to experiencing heaven in this world is through the Jesus Prayer."

INNER WORLD AND OUTER WORLD

We can divide the reality into the inner world and the outer world. The inner world comprises everything that exists in one's mind and heart, including thoughts, memories, mental activities, feelings, and one's physical body. The outer world consists of everything else around us. The physical body, equipped with physical senses, acts as the gateway between the inner world and the outer world.

Prayer as Surrender to God

Many people believe that they will find peace and happiness if everything goes right for them in the outer world. They believe that if they get the right job, have the right income, obtain the right degree, find the right partner, live in the right house, drive the right car, wear the right clothes, own the right watch or handbag, wear the right kind of jewelry, go on holiday to the right location with the right people, get their child admitted to the right school, and so on, they will automatically be happy and at peace. However, when things don't go as planned, they often become disappointed and blame others or themselves. They try even harder to change the outer world, thinking that happiness is just around the corner and that the key to peace and contentment lies in getting things right in the outer world.

The key to inner peace and happiness is not found outside but within ourselves. To attain a state of calm and contentment, it is important to examine and adjust our thoughts, beliefs, attitudes, and expectations toward people and things in the outer world. The power to achieve inner peace and happiness lies within us rather than in the hands of some powerful individuals or unknown forces that exist out there. This is a liberating idea as it highlights our capacity for agency and the freedom to choose.

Undoubtedly, we are all called to work toward positive changes in the outside world. This could involve protecting ourselves or our loved ones from an abusive relationship, or working toward reducing poverty, injustice, and suffering in the world. However, it is important to recognize that our external behavior often reflects what is happening inside of us. Therefore, it is wise to work toward inner peace before we attempt to bring about peace in the world.

The Jesus Prayer is a reliable bridge that helps us connect with our inner world and, with Christ's assistance, bring order and clarity to our lives. It serves as a gateway to the infinite source of love and life energy that can help us overcome obstacles, heal traumas, reduce stress, soothe pain, ease fears, unload worries, and banish temptations. By channeling the graces of Christ into our inner reality, the prayer facilitates the transformation of our inner world, leading to inner peace, joy, and happiness. Ultimately, it is the Holy Spirit praying within us and transforming us into a fitting home for Christ.

The Jesus Prayer focuses on changing us from within rather than changing the outer world to suit our preferences. This process involves a long journey of transformation, purification, and healing, which ultimately enables us to become channels of Christ's healing love and compassion for others. Significantly, the prayer has a direct impact on our ego or our fallen self. It undoes the ego's defenses and destroys its working mechanisms. As a result, many people experience strong inner resistance when practicing the Jesus Prayer. This resistance is the ego fighting for its survival against the purifying effects of the prayer on the soul.

HUMAN NATURE: GOOD OR EVIL?

During the period between the fourth and second centuries BCE, Chinese philosophers debated whether human nature is inherently good or bad. Different scholars offered different answers, and most prominent among them were Mencius and Han Fei Tzu. According to Mencius, who belonged to the Confucianist school, human nature is essentially good. People are born with four foundational virtues, namely, humaneness, righteousness, propriety, and wisdom.[1] The cultivation of these virtues is the basis of education and human development. On the other hand, Han Fei Tzu, who was part of the Legalist school, believed that human nature is inherently evil. Therefore, social order must be maintained through the rule of law.[2] The ruler, who has the authority (*shih*), governs the people by enforcing laws. Unlike the Confucianist's view, the ruler does not have to be a virtuous person who is exemplary in good conduct but someone who has the authority to reward and punish those who comply or disobey the laws.

Prayer as Surrender to God

As Christians, how do we respond to the question of whether human nature is inherently good or evil? The answer is both. According to Christianity, humans are good by nature because we were created by a good God, in God's own image and likeness. Therefore, we have a great potential for goodness within us. However, Christianity also teaches that humans have fallen into sin, and there is a strong inclination toward evil in us. This means that the capacity for good and the propensity for evil coexist in us, even among baptized Christians.

St. Paul's letter to the Romans, in chapter 7, provides an accurate description of the inner conflict that exists within the human soul. In this passage, St. Paul identifies two opposing forces that coexist within each of us. On one hand, it is our inmost self (or true self) that delights in the law of God, desires to do good, and hates what is evil. On the other hand, it is the fallen self (or ego) that delights in evil and opposes the law of God. St. Paul emphasizes that the domination of evil in the human soul is significant and that the human will is incapable of doing good by its own power. In fact, St. Paul describes this domination of evil in the human soul as *slavery to sin*. The way we are rescued from this slavery is by God's grace through faith in Jesus Christ.

When we pray the Jesus Prayer earnestly and persistently, it has the power to target directly our fallen self, break down its defenses, and destroy its working mechanisms through a process of purification. As our fallen self is a dwelling place of the evil spirit, the purification process not only diminishes the fallen self but also eliminates the agents of darkness from our soul. It rescues us from the wretched state of being held captive to the power of darkness. The prayer brings the saving grace of our Lord Jesus Christ into our body, soul, heart, and mind to free us from slavery to sin. We are not alone in our inner struggles as we have a powerful ally in Jesus Christ, who helps and guides us in this war against the agents of darkness. Once Jesus takes part in this inner conflict, there is an accelerating victory of light over darkness and good over evil. Once darkness is exposed to the light and dispelled, we are liberated from its tyrannical rule. We become freer, simpler, and more consistent in thinking, feeling, and acting. Our true self is free to do good unhindered by the agents of darkness. Our divided will, which results from the Fall, is healed. We return to the original simplicity and unity by divine grace through the Jesus Prayer.

This is not to say that our inner struggle is over once and for all. We experience progressive stages of liberation when the power of the Lord's name overcomes the tyrannical rule of darkness within us. After the first experience of liberation, the inner struggle continues, but generally with less intensity. It requires constant vigilance and prayers against the evil one. The enemy will always try to intervene, to take control again, time after time. This is why we must *pray without ceasing* (1 Thess 5:17), or in the words of Jesus, "Stay awake and pray" (Matt 26:41).

To sum up, the Jesus Prayer helps purify the soul by breaking down the ego's defenses and destroying its working mechanism, which eliminates the influence of the evil spirit. That is why the ego and the bad spirit strongly detest the Jesus Prayer and would fight frantically to prevent us from reciting it.

INNER RESISTANCE TO THE JESUS PRAYER

As human beings, we often experience an inner struggle between our desire to follow God's calling and our urge to be in charge of our own lives. On the one hand, we long to be close to God and experience a strong connection with him; on the other hand, we want to maintain control and have things our way. It is often fear that keeps us from coming closer to God. It is the fear of our unworthiness in God's sight, therefore, the fear of God's rejec-

Prayer as Surrender to God

tion. It is the unconscious fear that getting closer to God might rob us of our freedom and independence, which can be a significant obstacle on our spiritual journey and hinder our prayer life. Although people may claim to want to draw closer to God, fear often prevents them from doing so. Like an army commander, we battle fiercely against God to defend our freedom and self-determination.

For many of us Christians, the biggest hurdle to prayer is not a lack of knowledge but rather the intense resistance within us against prayer. Ultimately, this resistance reflects our reluctance to allow God into our lives. We want to maintain control over our lives, and we are not willing to let go without a fight. To put it in the words of St. Paul, it is not us but rather the sin that dwells within us that resists God. It is our fallen self and sinfulness within us that resist God and discourage us from praying.

Our resistance to prayer can also originate from doubts about God's existence or goodness. Many people have distorted images of God in their minds, fearing that if God knew more about them, God would punish them or abandon them. This can seem too painful to bear, so they avoid God and try to do things without God. Others fear that if they become friends with God, God will send suffering to them. They are not sure if they can become vulnerable by entrusting themselves to God. These distorted images of God keep many people from deep personal encounters and intimacy with God.

We can also feel strong resistance to the Jesus Prayer when we are in spiritual desolation. We might be overwhelmed by a sense of unworthiness, banished by God, trapped in the pit of sin, and unable to get out. In that situation, reciting the Jesus Prayer makes us feel uncomfortable, restless, uneased, and seemingly without benefit. That is why many people give up reciting the prayer.

The key to overcoming our inner resistance while reciting the Jesus Prayer is *perseverance*. To overcome our inner resistance, we

THE BREATH OF CHRIST

need to gather all our convictions and efforts and recite each word earnestly, even if it is uncomfortable or challenging. Like a patient who drinks bitter medicine they know will cure them, our goal is to overcome everything within us that resists the prayer, believing that the prayer is the remedy we need. The more resistance we feel against the prayer, the more effort we must put into overcoming it. The result is the victory of Christ over our fallen self, God's grace over sin, and light over darkness. We experience freedom, lightness, joy, peace, and a new sense of aliveness and connection with God.

It can be helpful if we name the resistance in us and turn it into prayer. For example:

- *Lord, I feel very uncomfortable reciting the prayer because I don't want to lose my independence. Lord Jesus, help me!*
- *Lord, I want to be in charge and not lose control over my life. Lord Jesus, help me!*
- *Lord Jesus, every time I pray, I feel uneasy because I am afraid you might punish me or send me suffering. Lord Jesus, help me!*
- *Lord, I feel like I am in a pit of sin and filth. I feel that I am being banished from you. I feel very unworthy of you. Lord Jesus, help me!*
- *Lord, it feels so uncomfortable reciting this prayer. Lord Jesus, help me! Lord Jesus, help me!*

In some cases, people feel a very strong resistance to the Jesus Prayer even though they really need it. Reciting the prayer can feel so unsettling that they would not want to do it at all. In these cases, if you are a prayer companion or spiritual guide, it is helpful to be patient, stay at their side, and recite the prayer with them. It would be of even greater benefit to help them name their inner resistance and turn it into prayer, as suggested here.

Prayer as Surrender to God

A DIVERSITY OF SPIRITUAL BENEFITS AND EXPERIENCES

St. Gregory of Sinai writes at length about the fruits of the Jesus Prayer and how to distinguish them from other inner movements. He explains that the energy of the Holy Spirit received in baptism is realized in two ways: through the practice of commandments and the continuous invocation of the Lord Jesus under spiritual guidance. The first way manifests more slowly than the second, which manifests more quickly but requires diligence and perseverance. He then describes the fruits of the prayer: warmth and joy in the intellect, love for God and neighbors inflamed in the heart, outpouring of humility and contrition.[3] As Gregory points out, it is the activity of the Holy Spirit praying in us that brings about these fruits, not just our activity. To pray the Jesus Prayer is to give ourselves to the Holy Spirit's redeeming activity in us. Through perseverance over time, this divine activity brings about a total transformation of our being when the seed of grace received at baptism grows and bears fruit.

There is a natural progression of experience as the divine energy reaches the depths of one's soul. Gregory writes, "To start with it rises like a fire of joy from the heart; in the end it is like light made fragrant by divine energy."[4] The experience of praying the Jesus Prayer varies from one person to another, depending on their current state:

> In some it appears as awe arising in the heart, in others as a tremulous sense of jubilation, in others as joy, in others as joy mingled with awe, or as tremulousness mingled with joy, and sometimes it manifests itself as tears and awe. For the soul is joyous at God's visitation and mercy, but at the same time is in awe and trepidation at His presence because it is guilty of so many sins.[5]

THE BREATH OF CHRIST

Gregory's description of the signs of the Holy Spirit at work reflects the intricate nature of the human soul. The soul experiences God's saving action as joy and also as tremulousness or trepidation. Made in God's image and likeness, the soul rejoices in God's presence as it recognizes the one who fulfills its deepest longings. At the same time, the ego, engrossed in delusion and sin, reacts with revulsion and trepidation as it recognizes the divine action through which God claims dominion in its little kingdom. The false self fights against the Jesus Prayer for fear of losing control over the inner world. This is because the Jesus Prayer specifically targets the false self and its numerous displays, chipping away its defenses, exposing its falsehood and delusions, and nullifying its efforts to validate itself through gaining possession of things or control of others. Whether the soul is relatively free or under the grip of the false self, the effect of the Jesus Prayer can be dominantly joyous or sorrowful. Gregory continues:

> Again, in some the soul at the outset experiences an unutterable sense of contrition and an indescribable pain....For the living and active Logos—that is to say, Jesus—penetrates, as the apostle says, to the point at which soul separates from body, joints from marrow (cf. Heb. 4:12), so as to expel by force every trace of passion from both soul and body.[6]

In the early stages of purification, there is often tremendous resistance to the Jesus Prayer. The indescribable pain signifies the ego fighting desperately to hold on to life or negotiate a compromise. The Jesus Prayer actively connects the living Christ with our inner reality, where all our shadows, weaknesses, sinfulness, and falsehoods are exposed to the divine presence. With diligent and persistent practice of the prayer, the living Christ, as the divine healer, reaches more deeply into one's psyche to bring about more complete healing and transformation. At first, the Jesus Prayer feels like the experience of a deep clean. With perseverance in the

Prayer as Surrender to God

prayer practice, it feels like a total demolition and reconstruction of the whole person: body, mind, heart, and soul, from the inside out. In effect, it is the process through which one's inner world is repurposed into a suitable home for the living Christ.

> In others it is manifest as an unconquerable love and peace, shown toward all, or as a joyousness that the fathers have often called exultation—a spiritual force and an impulsion of the living heart that is also described as a vibration and sighing of the Spirit who makes wordless intercession for us to God (cf. Rom. 8:26). Isaiah has also called this the "waves" of God's righteousness (cf. Isa. 48:18), while the great Ephrem calls it "spurring." The Lord Himself describes it as "a spring of water welling up for eternal life" (John 4:14)—He refers to the Spirit as water—a source that leaps up in the heart and erupts through the ebullience of its power.[7]

For a soul more fittingly disposed to the divine activity, the Jesus Prayer brings about favorable fruits such as love, peace, joy, or exultation. The terms used by Gregory indicate significant movements in the body, heart, and spirit noticeable by practitioners: "spiritual force," "impulsion of the heart," "vibration," "sighing of the Spirit," "waves of God's righteousness," "spurring," and "spring of water welling up." These tangible signs signify the Holy Spirit at work in the soul as one recites the Jesus Prayer with the right attitude and intention. Gregory also distinguishes various kinds of exultation, joyousness, awe, and trembling. He also points out two different forms of energy at work in beginners: one from grace, the other from delusion. On the divine energy, he writes:

> The energy of grace is the power of spiritual fire that fills the heart with joy and gladness, stabilizes, warms and purifies the soul, temporarily stills our provocative thoughts, and for a time suspends the body's impulsions. The signs and fruits

that testify to its authenticity are tears, contrition, humility, self-control, silence, patience, self-effacement and similar qualities, all of which constitute undeniable evidence of its presence.[8]

Gregory helpfully describes the effects of the energy of grace on the heart, soul, and mind, as well as the tangible signs that can authenticate its divine origin. On the other hand, the energy of delusion is the sinful passion for sexual pleasure. Its effects on the soul are "mindless joy, presumption and confusion, accompanied by a mood of ill-defined sterile levity, and fomenting above all the soul's appetitive power with its sensuality."[9] Gregory points out that this sinful passion nourishes itself on pleasure and is aided by the insatiable belly. If one gives in to its temptations, it inflames the soul and draws it more and more to self-indulgence while all grace is expelled from the person.[10]

Apart from these pointers, Gregory also explains how we can discern whether the inner movement is from God or from the enemy. He repeats the fruits of true prayer: warmth of the heart, scorification of the passions, joy and delight in the soul, unwavering love and unhesitating certainty. The key to discernment, as Gregory points out, is whether the soul accepts a movement with "unhesitating certainty" or with doubt. He writes, "The holy fathers teach that if the heart is in doubt about whether to accept something either sensory or conceptual that enters the soul, then that thing is not from God but has been sent by the devil."[11] As Gregory explains, what is from God feels natural to the soul and congruent with its holy aspirations. In contrast, what is from the enemy can be detected through discernment even though it might come under clever disguises. For instance, the enemy can substitute unruly heat for spiritual warmth, mindless joy, and a muggy sense of pleasure for spiritual delight, thereby leading the soul to self-satisfaction and vanity.

A person of experience and discernment will be able to distinguish between what comes from God and what comes from the enemy by the "taste" it leaves in the soul. "As the palate discriminates between different kinds of food (cf. Eccles. 36:18, 19), so the spiritual sense of taste clearly and unerringly reveals everything as it truly is."[12] To put it differently, our soul has its own taste buds that can distinguish between God's activity and the enemy's activity. With practice over time, this spiritual sense can be sharpened to help the soul follow God's promptings and protect itself from the enemy's deceits.

WHICH PRAYER FORMULA SHOULD I USE?

If you are wondering which formula of the Jesus Prayer to use, it is good to try out different options to see how they resonate with you. From my experience, each prayer formula vibrates in us differently, like each string of a cello generates its own vibration frequency in the chamber of the instrument. The right formula is one that resonates deeply in us, to the core of our being, each time we recite with reverence and intention. At the same time, there are powerful forces in us that resist the invocation of the Lord's name. The forces of resistance, which come from our fallen self and the enemy, are most acutely felt when we begin this prayer practice. This inner resistance to the Jesus Prayer can manifest as boredom, discomfort, sleepiness, loss of interest, distracting thoughts, or doubt about whether this prayer is helpful or suitable. Many Christians have "tried" various formulae of the Jesus Prayer but quickly gave up because of this inner resistance. They might feel bored, distracted, sleepy, or uncomfortable when they recite one prayer formula, so they use another formula. But this second formula also generates similar effects, perhaps to a different degree, so they change to another formula, and so on. Before long, they feel that no formula is suitable for them, so they give up.

THE BREATH OF CHRIST

Regarding which formula to use, I suggest three things. First, for beginners, it is good to choose one formula and persevere with it. Second, the practitioner needs to be intentional about overcoming their inner resistance to the prayer. When we encounter difficulties in this prayer practice, the temptation is to change to a different formula or to give up. The answer to our difficulties is to persevere with the same formula in the same prayer practice. With determination and perseverance, we will find that the prayer becomes easier to recite, and we will experience the spiritual fruits St. Gregory wrote about, namely warmth, awe, joy, contrition, tears, and so on. Third, the review of prayer afterward is crucial. St. Ignatius of Loyola emphasizes the importance of reviewing our prayer because we can gain valuable insights by looking back at our prayer experience. For some, keeping a spiritual diary is helpful in the review of prayer. We can record a prayer formula we use, its effects on us as we recite it, and any signs of resistance, such as discomfort, boredom, distraction, doubt, sleepiness, or the urge to change the formula or give up. Once we can name these from reviewing our prayer, it becomes clear what we should do next. We can also share our review of prayer with a spiritual guide.

As the Jesus Prayer makes Jesus a living presence in us and transforms our whole being into a suitable abode for him, it is no wonder that our fallen self would rebel and the enemy would try many things to stop us from reciting it. The key to overcoming all obstacles is *perseverance*. We have endless access to the Lord's efficacious graces through the invocation of his name. We simply have to keep doing it constantly as we face endless challenges in life.

3

Turning Our Feeling into Prayer

After participating in a group retreat on the Jesus Prayer, Kim wrote, "I learned to speak to Jesus as with a friend who is always at my side and ask for his help by saying, Lord Jesus, help me! I experienced a peace that I have never experienced before…without fear, anxiety, or regret. The burdens of the past become much lighter and fade from memory. Today is the beginning of a new chapter. I feel liberated from the worries about the future because God has planned it all for me. What is left is the present moment. God has given me life, with every breath and heartbeat…as part of God's creation. I choose to live in the present because I know God is with me only in the present moment. I surrender to the Lord and am delighted to invite the Lord into my soul as his home."

NAME OUR FEELINGS

In the previous chapters, we discussed the history and standard forms of the Jesus Prayer, how to recite it, the difficulties one might face, and the fruits of the prayer. This chapter provides an explanation of the approach I propose in this book and have outlined in chapter 1.

THE BREATH OF CHRIST

The Jesus Prayer is focused on the inner world—our mind and heart—where the grace of God can bring about personal transformation. Our inner world is the realm of thoughts and emotions, which we tend to overlook while attending to the endless demands of the outer world. Many people struggle to articulate their feelings and, therefore, have limited capacity to understand and manage them. Recent research highlights the significance of emotions in both personal and professional contexts. For instance, studies indicate that feeling happy, calm, confident, focused, enthusiastic, or hopeful can lead to comfort within ourselves and enable us to perform physical and mental tasks at our best. On the other hand, when we feel upset, irritable, impatient, angry, fearful, or anxious, we may become uncomfortable with our emotions, and our performance can be impaired. If these emotional states persist for extended periods, they can adversely affect our health and impact our relationships with others.[1]

My proposed approach involves naming our emotions and turning them into prayers by invoking the Lord's name. This practice has significant psychological and spiritual benefits. Spiritually, it helps foster an intimate relationship with Jesus by inviting him into every aspect of our lives, sharing with him each of our thoughts, emotions, worries, and burdens that we carry. This method helps us pray by describing where we are at any moment and then turning it into prayer. It helps us remember Jesus and pray to him whenever, wherever, and however we find ourselves. It makes Jesus present to us in the here and now. Or, more accurately, it makes us more present to Jesus here and now.

Psychologically, naming our emotions can benefit us in five ways: it helps to (1) bring awareness into our inner world, (2) integrate the information flow in our brains, (3) soothe the hyperactive limbic system and bring balance to our brain activities, (4) externalize our emotions, and (5) give us choices over how we respond. The acronym might be helpful: AISEC—Awareness,

Turning Our Feeling into Prayer

Integration, Soothing, Externalization, and Choice. Let's look at these in some detail.

First, naming our emotions helps bring awareness into our inner world. Psychiatrist Dr. Daniel Siegel relates the story of Stuart, a highly intellectual man disconnected from his feelings. The first step in his journey to integration and a more enjoyable marital relationship involved tuning in to his body's signals and the imagery that arose from them. These exercises help him gain awareness of his inner world as he becomes more and more able to sense and describe what is happening inside.[2]

Second, naming our emotions helps integrate information flow from diverse parts of our brains. As Dr. Siegel explains, using words to describe and name things is the function of the language center of the left hemisphere cortex. To answer the question, "How am I feeling?" we use our left hemisphere's linguistic faculty to decode the words of the question and send a message across the corpus callosum (the bridge between the left and right hemispheres) to activate the right hemisphere, which comes up with the nonverbal somatic-sensory data corresponding to feelings. A brain signal then returns in the reverse direction, from the right brain through the corpus callosum to the language center of the left hemisphere cortex, where this neural information is turned into words.[3] If this process is repeated many times through noticing and naming our feelings, neural pathways will be strengthened between our left and right hemispheres. We become more attuned to our inner world and can be more in tune with the emotional states of others.

Third, naming our emotions can help soothe the reactive limbic firing and bring balance to our inner world. As Dr. Siegel points out, people with excess right-mode flow and overactive feelings can suffer from emotional dysregulation and chaotic outbursts. Simply noticing and naming one's feelings in such cases can help bring balance by providing a mental distance in the sanctuary of the left brain. Research has shown that naming an emotion can soothe limbic firing.[4] In other words, we need to "name it to tame it" by using the left language centers to calm the excessive firing of the right emotional areas, thereby bringing balance to our mental activities.

Fourth, naming our emotions helps externalize them by excising them from who we are. We are often lost in the flow of our emotions and become one with them. There is no distance between who I am and how I feel. As Dr. Siegel puts it:

> Our ability to "represent" an emotional reaction to ourselves, to give it a name and a meaning, helps to lift us out of the immediacy of an experience so that we can respond to it effectively. Knowing that our minds regulate the flow of energy and information enables us to feel the reality of these two forms of mental experience—and then act on them rather than get lost in them.[5]

Through externalization, we can look at an emotion objectively as something *out there* rather than an integral part of who we are. A safe distance is created between us and our emotions. Fifth, we can choose how we respond when we can externalize our emotions. Once in this safe space, we can respond thoughtfully to the person or situation rather than react out of impulse or habit.

In summary, by noticing and naming our negative emotions, we can step back from them, reflect, and choose a thoughtful response. This practice can bring us awareness, integration, soothing, balance, and choice. By acknowledging and naming our emotions, we can turn them into prayer and invite the living Christ into our inner world. Christ becomes a faithful friend who is with us as we become aware of and integrate our emotions, which helps to soothe us and restore balance during times of emotional distress. This practice also allows us to formulate a thoughtful response to the situation at hand.

Turning Our Feeling into Prayer

ASKING FOR NOTHING ELSE

When people begin using this prayer method, as soon as they name their emotions, needs, and concerns, they are quickly drawn into petitions for changes in the external world, thereby losing their focus on the inner world and their relationship with Jesus. The practice of the Jesus Prayer—including this adapted form—is to make one petition only. That one petition to the Lord is, "*Have mercy on me!*" or "*Help me!*" For example, a man may name his concerns for his ailing mother as he prays, "*Lord, my mother is in hospital with fractures in her spine after a fall. She has a heart condition and is very frail. Lord Jesus, help me!*"

After saying this, he might be drawn to make other petitions for his mother, "*Lord, help my mother recover from her fractures. Help her sleep tonight. May she recover her strength and return home soon.*" These are prayers that petition for changes in the external world. While these petitions are good in themselves, they can quickly take our focus away from our inner world and our relationship with Jesus. To maintain our focus on that intimate relationship with Jesus, which is the source of our life and strength, we can rephrase these petitions as follows:

* *Lord, I am worried about my mother's injury and wish she recovers quickly from her fractures. Lord Jesus, help us!*
* *Lord, my mother has not been able to sleep for two nights. I wish that she could have a good night's sleep tonight. Lord Jesus, help us!*
* *Lord, I wish my mother recovers her strength and returns home soon. Lord Jesus, help us!*

These petition prayers are more focused on the person's relationship with Jesus, and on handing over to the Lord one's concerns and wishes. These are the most beautiful prayers, and I think also the most effective for oneself and one's ailing mother.

THE BREATH OF CHRIST

Consider the differences between the following:

1. *"Lord, help my mother recover quickly from her fractures."*
2. *"Lord, I wish my mother would recover quickly from her fractures. Lord Jesus, help us!"*

In (1), we ask Jesus to intervene to bring about a certain outcome for our loved one. In (2), we express our desire for a particular outcome and entrust ourselves and our loved one to his care. We place our faith more fully in Jesus and his divine plan, trusting that whatever Jesus does will be the best for our loved one. Implicitly, it states, *"Lord, I wish for a certain outcome for my mother, but I am not sure if it is in line with your holy will. I entrust my mother to you, confident you will know what is best for her and how to help her. In that trust and confidence, I simply ask, Lord Jesus, help us!"*

It is similar to the situation when that man takes his injured mother to a hospital, he need not instruct the doctors on what to do for his mother. For example, he need not tell the doctors, "I think my mother has fractured some vertebrae. Please do some X-rays of her spine, immobilize her, and give her some analgesics." He simply needs to present the mother's ailments and ask the doctors to help her, trusting that they will know exactly what to do for her. When we come to Jesus, we can trust he will know exactly what to do for our loved ones. We can state our concerns and worries, our wishes for certain outcomes, and then we hand them over to Jesus, simply asking that he help us.

As we name our worries, concerns, and wishes and turn them into prayers, we experience lightness in the assurance that the Lord hears our concerns and shares our burdens. The prayer opens up new horizons in which the Lord is always attentive to our needs and those of our loved ones. These prayers bring our good wishes for our loved ones to God and entrust them to God's loving providence. They give us a sense of lightness, calmness,

Turning Our Feeling into Prayer

and rest from our worries and stress. After entrusting our needs and wishes to God's care, we then accept and adapt ourselves to whatever might come. As we grow in trust in the Lord, our petitions become simpler and more relational. We are more open and receptive to God's purposes and activities as we entrust more of our needs and those of our loved ones to God.

BRAVING THE INNER WORLD

For those who have experienced traumas in their lives, the inner world can be a dreadful wilderness where monsters lurk in the shadows. However, with Jesus as our companion and guide, our inner world becomes a safer place. By standing with Jesus, naming what we see, and turning them into prayers, we can access the most extraordinary power against those monsters and shadows by exposing them to the light. Monsters are shown to be no more than unprocessed past hurts, and shadows are nothing other than uncomfortable memories that the mind has suppressed to create a working space for daily activities. With Jesus constantly at our side, nothing in our inner world will be too much to handle. The journey into the inner world becomes an expedition with redemptive meaning.

As we invite Christ into our inner world, we allow the divine light to shine through the darkness, bringing life, healing, compassion, love, and peace into the chaos and fear present within us. With the Jesus Prayer, we form a new alliance with Jesus to reclaim for God what has been lost to the power of darkness. This process will bring peace to our anxious mind, heal our traumas, calm our anger, replace our inner critic with compassion, and help us let go of our resistance to the unchangeable realities of life. Simultaneously, the ego will dissolve as it is exposed more and more to the light. As our alliance reclaims more inner territory for God, we will feel a greater capacity for love and joy and lesser room for shame, anger, fear, and regret.

As Christians, many of us experience the ongoing conflict between light and darkness, love and fear, Christ and the ego, compassion and judgment in our inner world. Through perseverance in prayer, the grace of Christ will accelerate the triumph of light over darkness. The final victory is when Christ reclaims all of our inner world for God. All our thoughts, memories, understanding, and will now belong to God and are at God's disposal. We are in total union with Christ while the ego is totally dissolved. Our will is in union with God's will; our consciousness expands and becomes part of God's consciousness.

To use Pope Francis's metaphor, the *field hospital* where healing takes place is not only something external but also the internal realm of our thinking, judging, feeling, choosing, and acting in everyday life. This prayer method helps make God's gift of salvation more practical and tangible for Christians today. It is the Good News of salvation for our mind, heart, body, and soul. Starting from the next chapter, we will delve into psychology, neuroscience, and spiritual traditions to gain a deeper insight into the human mind and how the Jesus Prayer can bring Christ's divine assistance wherever we find ourselves.

SELF-KNOWLEDGE, COMPANION, LIGHT OF CONSCIOUSNESS

As we grow in the practice of this prayer, we grow in self-knowledge, intimacy with Jesus, and the intensity of our awareness.

First, we gain deeper self-knowledge as we are more attuned to our inner life with its feelings and thoughts and more able to moderate uncomfortable emotions as they arise. We also gain insight into the factors (from within and without) that can trigger cer-

Turning Our Feeling into Prayer

tain emotional states and what choices we can make to prevent a reactive meltdown. Once we become well acquainted with our inner life, we can identify the numerous unhealthy mental habits that take our vital energies and convert them to toxins that harm our mental and physical health. The Jesus Prayer helps us break those harmful habit loops and create a more peaceful and healthier inner world. With greater self-knowledge, we also grow in self-compassion, which in turn helps us become more compassionate with others.

Second, as we continually describe our inner world to Jesus and implore his assistance, we grow in intimacy with the Lord by making ourselves transparent and vulnerable to him. We let the Lord into the innermost corners of our being and share with him all the secrets of our lives, thoughts, feelings, and desires. Jesus becomes our companion and Savior in a very literal and tangible way. As we grow in intimacy with the Lord, we are no longer lonely but live in the abundance of peace and joy that he alone can offer.

Third, each time we share with the Lord our thoughts, emotions, wishes, or burdens, we add fuel to the light of our awareness. The more we practice this prayer, the brighter our light will be burning to illuminate more and more of our inner world. This prayer creates a safe distance between us and the things we can observe in our inner world: thoughts, emotions, desires, concerns, burdens, and wishes. Instead of being thrown back and forth by the endless waves in the hostile sea of life, we become observers reporting to Jesus what we see in our inner world. The more we observe and report to Jesus, the more we experience him as a living person at our side, and nothing in the inner or outer world can separate us from this secure base.

This approach to the Jesus Prayer is the interface between discursive prayer and contemplative prayer. It starts with our feelings and thoughts and then takes us to a trusting rest in the Lord. It engages with the thinking mind and leads us into silence beyond words and thoughts. It takes us ultimately into the restful and joyous union with the living Christ.

THE BREATH OF CHRIST: A PERSONAL JOURNEY

My own journey began when I chose a Vietnamese formula that resonated deeply with me and started reciting it. While attempting to link the Jesus Prayer with my breathing, I encountered strong inner resistance to the prayer, which I mentioned in chapter 1. I was able to overcome this resistance by persistently using the same prayer formula and breathing technique. During inhalation, I recited "Lord Jesus" while asking Jesus to fill my body, mind, and soul. And while exhaling, I recited "Help me," thereby letting go of any worries, stress, fear, or pain I was carrying. Despite feeling discomfort, doubt, sleepiness, and distractions, I persevered with the prayer.

After a few days, the resistance gave way, and I felt a tremendous sense of peace, lightness, and connection with Christ. Prayer became easier and brought great spiritual benefits to my mind, body, and soul. This moment was a significant turning point in my life, as I felt I had gained a faithful companion in Christ. Reciting the prayer would quickly and reliably fill me with peace and joy. I had a new sense of calmness and connection that I had never experienced on a consistent basis before. I even thought to myself at one point, "Even if I found myself in hell, reciting this prayer would make it bearable."

In 2011, my godson faced difficulties adjusting to life in a new city. As a result, I offered him some guidance on prayer that involved naming one's feelings and asking the Lord for assistance. After introducing my godson to this form of prayer, I began using it consistently in my own prayer life, and it proved to be a great help. It turned out that the Lord wanted me to learn this prayer

Turning Our Feeling into Prayer

method and experience its benefits. I discovered that by using this prayer method, I could turn my anxiety, worries, fears, and stress into prayer, which led to a sense of peace and joy. At one point, I was thrilled to realize that I could *choose* how I felt. This method of prayer helped me get through my doctoral studies.

What I wrote to my godson later became the basis of an article on the Jesus Prayer, which I then shared with members of the Vietnamese Christian Life Community in Worcester, Massachusetts. Before long, I shared it with seminarians during formation workshops and Jesuits in different stages of formation. I also used it widely in parish retreats, individually directed retreats, guided group retreats, and in the context of spiritual direction.

There was a time when the prayer felt like bread from heaven. With each breath, I felt like I was receiving the living Christ into my body. Breathing while thinking of Christ gave me tremendous joy throughout my body, as though every cell rejoiced when it came into contact with Christ's presence. This joy accompanied the awareness of the breath starting in my upper airway, going into my lungs and then radiating outward through my body. It was the experience of breathing Christ when my body came alive and danced wherever it was touched by Christ. It was an experience of union with Christ as described in John 6:56: "Those who eat my flesh and drink my blood abide in me, and I in them."

However, over a period of a few weeks, this feeling of joy and awe gradually disappeared. Christ assured me that I wasn't losing him but that he was inviting me to an even deeper level of union with him.

During the COVID lockdown, I did an eight-day retreat while staying home at my Jesuit community and talking with my spiritual guide over the phone. Throughout the retreat, I had a deep sense of Christ within me, most palpable in my abdominal region, which was the source of joy, peace, and contentment independent of everything happening around me. It was a time of walking in joy as I felt a connection with the divine presence within me. The breathing prayer no longer generated waves of joy throughout my body, but it helped me calm my mind and return to the center to be with the joy that was already within me.

Over a span of fourteen years, I faced various challenges that tested my commitment to this prayer. These challenges took the form of troubling doubts, questions, judgments, and even an attraction to other spiritual traditions and practices. Despite these challenges, I persisted with my prayer practice for long periods of time. However, there were also periods when I stopped this practice altogether, which could sometimes last for months or even over a year. But every time I returned to the practice, I found that the experience was just as easy and peaceful as it was the last time I practiced it.

During my six-month sabbatical in early 2022, I embarked on this book project, which has been a significant learning experience for me. As I delved deeper into the topics of anxiety, anger, trauma, and poor self-esteem, I gained a greater understanding of myself and how to use the prayer to invite Christ's presence more fully into my inner world. I was amazed to discover how healthcare professionals have incorporated mindfulness techniques to help individuals dealing with anxiety, anger, and trauma. Equally astonishing is that the Jesus Prayer can be applied in each of these situations.

THE BOUNDLESS DEPTHS OF THE JESUS PRAYER

After fourteen years of learning and practice, I discovered that there is no limit to the depths of the Jesus Prayer, just as there is no limit to the depths of God's salvation in Christ. Once you use the Jesus Prayer as the door to the living Christ, there is no limit to what Christ can do for you.

Nevertheless, there are certain limits to the Jesus Prayer that

Turning Our Feeling into Prayer

you might encounter. These limits are not imposed by God but rather by us humans, or more precisely, by our ego. Here is a list of things that can limit or render the Jesus Prayer ineffective:

1. Initial resistance to the prayer can be experienced as boredom, unease, distractions, sleepiness, doubts, or physical discomfort. To overcome this resistance, we simply persist with the same form of the prayer until the effects subside.
2. Reciting the Jesus Prayer on "automatic pilot" is not effective. Neuroscience shows that we switch to automatic pilots when performing familiar tasks to save energy and focus on more important tasks. For example, when riding a bicycle on a familiar route, we perform many tasks instinctively, like balancing our weight on the bike, applying force on one foot while relaxing the other, and watching out for people and moving vehicles. This allows our minds to concentrate on significant matters, like planning a shopping list or organizing dinner.

    When it comes to the Jesus Prayer, reciting it purely on automatic pilot is not effective. Over time, as we recite it frequently enough, the prayer largely becomes a habit. Yet for the prayer to bear fruit, we need to pay at least some attention to the invocation of the Lord's name. Note the importance of the appropriate sense of reverence in pleading for the Lord's assistance. Remember that the prayer is primarily a relationship with the Lord, not a way to get what we want.
3. Using prayer as a means to attain our goals is not acceptable. When we use prayer as a means to pursue a goal, we are serving our ego. This includes material and spiritual goals such as money, recognition, power, success, spiritual powers, knowledge, or enlightenment. There are two major problems with this approach. First, using the Lord's

THE BREATH OF CHRIST

name in the service of our ego is blasphemy. Second, it is wrong to expect that the Lord will abandon his will to do our will. We must not abuse the efficacy of the Jesus Prayer and treat it as a magic formula to obtain whatever we want.

As you learn to bring Christ's presence more deeply into your inner world, may you experience for yourself the boundless riches of God's gifts in Christ.

4

Unloading Our Burdens

Turning Anxiety into Prayer

Sophie has been referred to me for consultation regarding a bioethical issue. When we meet, she speaks of her intense longing for a child at this stage in her life; she is cohabitating with her partner, and she wants utilize assisted reproductive technologies. It is stressful for her because, having just turned forty, she feels her chances of mothering a child are slipping away. As she starts talking about her desire for a child, there is so much anxiety, tension, frustration, and distress regarding her current life situation. There are tears of pain that stem from a deep yearning. There is frustration and disgust with some aspects of her life. There is anxiety and stress regarding the obstacles and challenges she perceives on the path to parenthood. Then, there are Church laws against certain forms of assisted reproductive technologies. Sophie carries such heavy burdens and is visibly distressed by the tensions in her life.

Sophie's primary question to me is what she should do. As a spiritual director and ethicist, my task is to guide and empower Sophie to make her own decision. This involves explaining to her the pros and cons of various forms of reproductive technologies and exploring which course of action would be most fitting for her. Theoretically, a good decision would be consistent with her beliefs, values, and commitments. If she holds competing values and commitments, she must choose those with which she most identifies. This is what ethicists refer to as the exercise of one's autonomy.

As I listen to her story, I sense that Sophie cannot make a meaningful decision without dealing with the anxiety and worries that she is carrying. She needs to be in a better space to see what beliefs, values, and commitments are most important to her. She needs to unload her burdens before she can commit to a particular course of action. To do that, she needs sufficient mental working space to discern various options. What Sophie needs, first of all, is to unclutter her mind to create that mental working space.

I suggest to Sophie that we pray together, to which she agrees. I assist Sophie in naming her longing, worries, and distress, then turn them into prayer by invoking Jesus's name. Within minutes, Sophie experiences the power of Jesus's name and discovers a new support base for her life. We shall return to this later in the chapter.

RECOGNIZING ANXIETY

When I was growing up in Vietnam, Dad's favorite book was the Vietnamese translation of Dale Carnegie's bestselling *How to Stop Worrying and Start Living*.[1] Dad and Mum had many things to worry about when they took their nine young children and moved from Saigon to a farming village to start a new life in late 1975. Dad had worked as a public servant in South Vietnam during the war, and with the new government's constant urging for Saigon residents to leave the city and move to the New Economic Zones, Dad thought it was better to move early to a place of one's choice rather than staying and facing an uncertain future. Without any farming experience, my parents tried to raise a young family by growing corn and casava on one hectare of land on a hill about an hour's walk from home. My younger sister died at eight years of age from diphtheria, only a few months after we moved, due

Unloading Our Burdens

to a lack of medical care. My younger brother died of congenital heart disease three years later. There was very little income from the farm produce; we lived on the savings from selling the house in Saigon. Mum figured out that we could never live on the farm produce alone, so she went into the trading business to support the family. However, trading in farm produce across the provinces at the time certainly involved enormous risks. The police and local security guards were always on the watch for "illegal traders" of rice, beans, corn, tea leaves, and the like. Our livelihood could be ruined if Mum got caught with a large shipment. So a significant part of Mum's business was to figure out how to evade the authorities' watchful eye as she bought and moved the goods across the provinces on public transport. It would be correct to say I was brought up by anxious parents! So were millions of other children across the country at that time.

Fast forward to 1989: I lived in Australia with my three brothers, each of us having escaped from Vietnam by boat and spending some months in a refugee camp before being accepted for settlement in Australia. I was in my second year of medical school and attended psychology classes, which I enjoyed. When I learned the symptoms and signs of anxiety, I noticed them in myself for the first time and started putting the pieces together. I noticed my sweaty palms, palpitations, and nervousness during the anatomy tutorials when students were put on the spot and grilled about the various body parts and their functions. I noticed similar anxiety during exams and how too much of it could impair my performance.

Psychiatrists suggest that many of us are anxious without knowing it. It was certainly true for me until I discovered that I had most of the textbook symptoms of anxiety. Being as young and energetic as I was, I had thought anxiety was what my parents and other people had, not me. After Dad died in Vietnam, Mum and my younger sister migrated to Australia on the family reunion program. My siblings and I were well aware of Mum's anxiety and often tried our best to manage our issues without telling her, lest she worry. I learned much later that family members of an anxious person commonly adopt strategies to protect the anxious person from worries, as my siblings and I did with Mum. While it was easy to see anxiety in Mum, it was much harder to recognize it in myself. I took those uneasy feelings and apprehensions I had about the future for granted—they were just a part of life. Once I learned to recognize anxiety, I found that I am very prone to feeling anxious. I identified several triggers: academic writing, attending certain social gatherings, or presenting to an academic audience.

Psychology distinguishes between fear and anxiety. Fear is the emotional response to a real or perceived present threat. In contrast, anxiety is the emotional response in anticipation of a future threat.[2] Fear is typically associated with physical, cognitive, and behavioral features: physical arousal necessary for fight or flight, thoughts of imminent danger, and escape behaviors. Anxiety is often associated with muscle tension, vigilance toward a future threat, and cautious or avoidant behaviors.

Anxiety is also distinct from worry, though anxiety and worry often go together. Anxiety is a *feeling* of nervousness or agitation about a future threat. Worry is a *mental activity* in an attempt to solve a future issue that contains a degree of uncertainty.[3] The *Diagnostic and Statistical Manual of Mental Disorders, Fifth Edition* (DSM-5, the standard manual used by mental health professionals) refers to worry simply as "apprehensive expectation," which highlights the dread that accompanies the act of worrying. Worry, in fact, plays a vital role in the perpetuation of anxiety, to which we shall return.

Anxiety is the most common feature of our age. The majority of us across the globe are anxious people. The COVID-19 pandemic has induced even greater anxiety and stress in us. Many of us worry about infection risks, food availability, job security, work and schooling, access to health services, vaccine availability, and other forms of disruption.

Unloading Our Burdens

However, anxiety is not necessarily a mental health issue. According to the *Oxford Handbook of Psychiatry*, anxiety is defined as

> a normal and adaptive response to stress and danger which is pathological if prolonged, severe, or out of keeping with the real threat of the external situation. Anxiety has two components: psychic anxiety, which is an affect characterized by arousal, apprehension, a sense of vulnerability, and dysphoria; and somatic anxiety in which there are bodily sensations of palpitations, sweating, dyspnoea, pallor, and abdominal discomfort.[4]

Let's examine the psychosomatic aspects of anxiety. It begins with the mind sensing an impending danger, which triggers a response in both the mind and body. To effectively tackle a threat, we need a certain level of arousal. However, excessive arousal can be counterproductive and hinder our ability to respond appropriately. It is helpful to think of a threshold. Up to a certain point, more arousal will result in better mental and physical performance, which we can refer to as "good anxiety." Once that threshold is exceeded, further arousal can negatively impact performance, which we can call "bad anxiety."[5] Good anxiety is what the *Oxford Handbook* considers normal and adaptive. It helps us rise to the challenge by engaging our knowledge and gifts for the task.

The *Oxford Handbook* considers bad anxiety to be pathological and describes it as prolonged, severe, and disproportionate to the actual threat. It is when one's performance of physical and mental tasks is impaired by too much arousal in response to danger. This is experienced as "freaking out" or being frozen by anxiety during exams or athletic or musical performances.

Bad anxiety is prevalent but difficult to detect in ourselves. When anxious, we often lose the capacity to observe ourselves and reflect on our experiences. Once anxiety takes hold, it dominates our minds and impairs our ability to think clearly and creatively. Our anxious minds go into survival mode, and we cannot think beyond our terror.[6] Anxiety kills joy, humor, creativity, and often productivity. An anxious mind cannot think straight or work effectively. It has no room for fun or play. It is consumed by a constant dread of an impending and often poorly defined terror. An anxious mind is in pain, and it tries desperately to think itself out of pain. However, unable to think clearly, it gets caught in the relentless, repetitive, and useless thought patterns (called worrying) that only result in more pain. The anxious mind is like a hurt animal that tries to run away from danger but gets caught in a mental maze, unable to get out. Once it gets on the treadmills of worry, the harder it tries, the more entangled and hurt it becomes.

Psychiatrist Dr. Judson Brewer maintains that anxiety is the root cause of many unhealthy habits such as excessive drinking, problem eating, smoking, and gambling.[7] Very often, we experience distress without recognizing anxiety as the cause. To cope with the discomfort of anxiety, we adopt a behavior such as drinking alcohol to distract or soothe ourselves. This behavior does provide some temporary relief from distress. This relief serves as a reward that reinforces the behavior and turns it into a habit.

ANXIETY: THE MIND'S FUTURE PROJECTION

Anxiety is born from the unique ability of the human mind to predict what might happen in the future based on what happened in the past.[8] This ability allows us to plan and prepare for future events to our advantage. Our mind needs sufficient information to make reliable predictions about what will happen to prepare for the future. When data is lacking, our mind runs various versions of what might happen based on what happened previously. Anxiety comes when the mind's prediction resonates

Unloading Our Burdens

with a difficult situation we have experienced or heard about. Where there is uncertainty about the future, the vigilant mind becomes anxious because uncertainty means possible danger or risk of getting hurt.

Carnegie's *How to Stop Worrying and Start Living* helpfully details stories of how people have conquered worry and provides some practical guidelines from real-life experiences.[9] I think these guidelines are as relevant today as they were seven decades ago when the book was written. I offer a paraphrase of the familiar sources of worries identified in the book and how to protect ourselves from them.

We worry when we think of the future and try to problem-solve things that are vague or uncertain in the future. When we face uncertainty about the future, our minds picture various scenarios, and we ask ourselves how we would respond in each case. For example, "What will happen if my husband loses his job?" "What happens to our business if there is another wave of COVID?" Problem-solving is well and good when our mind is free from anxiety and capable of clear thinking. But when facing uncertainty about the future, our minds quickly perceive danger and become anxious, especially when much is at stake. Once we are anxious, our minds fall into the maze of worrying and become hopeless at problem-solving. That is why future problems invariably appear far more intimidating than today's problems. Overthinking about the future is the chief cause of worry and anxiety. Carnegie suggests we live one day at a time and avoid stewing about the future.

We worry when we need to do some planning or problem-solving instead. In addition to the point above, the lack of planning and problem-solving on issues at hand can also be a source of worry. It is helpful to think of two distinct modes of mental activity: (1) problem-solving and (2) worrying. The anxious mind tends to worry endlessly without taking concrete steps to improve the situation. Carnegie suggests that each time we catch ourselves worrying, we need to switch to the problem-solving mode by asking simple questions: "What is the problem?" "What is the cause of the problem?" "What are all possible solutions to the problem?" "What solution do you suggest?"[10]

We worry when we ruminate on our loss or misfortune. These include things that happened in the past. Grief is a normal response to losing a loved one, livelihood, or property. When we are in grief, our minds engage in the critical task of revising our inner map and guidebook to account for the loss we experience so that we can go on with our lives. But our minds can get caught in the cycle of regret, resentment, or blame, often in an attempt to ensure that a similar thing will never happen to us again. Many misfortunes are beyond our control, and the only lesson we can learn is to accept them and get on with life. Carnegie relates several stories on how people overcome their melancholy by keeping busy instead of ruminating about their misfortune.

We worry when we mull over things beyond our power to change or revise. Many things are beyond our control: our childhood and upbringing, our family of origin, our ethnicity, our skin color, and things that happened in the past. Regarding things that cannot be otherwise, the more we rebel against them, the more we suffer. Carnegie suggests that we cooperate with the inevitable and accept what cannot be changed or revised.

We are anxious when we imagine horrible things happening to us, our loved ones, or our livelihood, no matter how unlikely those things are. Our imagination presents the scariest scenarios based on our experiences or what we have heard on the news or from other people. A mother, fueled by anxiety, waiting up at night for her daughter to come home often imagines the most horrible possible scenarios: accident, robbery, rape, murder, and so on. These thoughts generate more anxiety, which in turn fuels even more worry. Carnegie suggests that we use the law of averages to drive away our worries about things that are statistically very unlikely to happen.

When we try to get even with our enemies, we generate turmoil and

Unloading Our Burdens

pain for ourselves. When we hate our enemies and try to get even, our health and happiness suffer. Carnegie points to Jesus's teachings on forgiveness and love of one's enemies as effective forms of self-care. As Carnegie says, "We may not be saintly enough to love our enemies, but, for the sake of our own health and happiness, let's at least forgive them and forget them."[11]

We are distressed by other people's ingratitude. When we do something beautiful or generous for other people, we often expect some expression of gratitude. But this expectation is often the cause of distress, as it is natural for people to forget to be grateful. Carnegie suggests that if we expect ingratitude in such situations, we will not be disappointed. Instead of expecting gratitude from others, it would be better to cultivate gratitude in ourselves and our children.

We worry when we try to imitate others. We are all unique people with unique abilities and characteristics. We are not meant to be like other people. When we try to be someone else, we will be unhappy because we can never succeed in being anyone other than ourselves. We are meant to unashamedly be the persons we are and to bring our unique gifts into this world. Singers, writers, artists, actors, musicians, businesspeople—all have to learn this lesson, many through spectacular failures, before they are bold enough to be themselves and flourish. Carnegie suggests that we find ourselves and be ourselves instead of trying to imitate others.

We worry about people's criticism when we try to please them or are too concerned about people's approval. This is more common when we are in a new work environment or doing work requiring professionalism or creativity. People who lack confidence in themselves are often overly concerned about other people's approval. Seeking approval from others to validate one's worth is exhausting and stressful. Carnegie suggests that we simply do the very best we can and then put up an umbrella against the rain of criticism.

THE BREATH OF CHRIST

We become fatigued and worried when we overwork, have poor work habits, or have no enthusiasm for our work. Carnegie suggests that we develop good work habits, including adequate rest and relaxation, and put enthusiasm into our work to prevent fatigue and worry.

Besides these common sources of worry, psychologists also point to the root causes of anxiety many of us carry in our psyche. Past trauma can be a source of anxiety when a situation triggers a sense of terror similar to what we experienced in the past. Self-hatred can be a hidden cause of performance anxiety when our self-image is incompatible with the task at hand.[12] These deep psychological issues need to be addressed within a safe environment with expert support.

ANXIETY AND THE HABIT LOOP

In *The Power of Habit*, Charles Duhigg explains the habit loop and its three components: cue, routine, and reward.[13] The reward-based learning process leads to automatic behavior that saves energy and frees up our minds for other tasks. Understanding how habits are formed can help us break bad habits and develop better ones. This insight has significant implications for treating addictions and anxiety.[14]

Building on the reward-based learning model, Brewer suggests that many addictions are formed as a way to cope with anxiety.[15] Here, anxiety triggers a behavior that turns into addiction through the habit loop. Since our mind is uncomfortable with the feeling of anxiety, it adopts a certain behavior to soothe or distract itself from the discomfort. If the behavior provides some relief from anxiety, this relief serves as a reward to reinforce the behavior over time. For instance, when a person feels anxious about an upcoming deadline (trigger), he lights a cigarette (behavior)

Unloading Our Burdens

and feels some relief from anxiety (result). This relief is a reward that reinforces the smoking behavior the next time he feels anxious. Over time, smoking becomes a habit that is triggered by anxiety. Each time he feels anxious, he craves a smoke and reaches for his cigarette without thinking about it. Addiction to alcohol, gambling, pornography, or heroin can develop through this exact mechanism. Brewer also suggests that everyday addictions such as shopping, computer gaming, eating, and social media can be formed in response to anxiety.[16] Knowing how habits and addictions develop in response to anxiety is immensely valuable for therapeutic interventions.

OBSERVING THE ANXIOUS THOUGHTS: MINDFULNESS MEDITATION

Mindfulness meditation brings focus to the present moment, disrupting anxiety and worry to provide a sense of calm and renewed energy. Popular apps like Headspace and Calm offer guided meditation, which shifts attention from worrying to observing one's body, feelings, and thinking, providing relief from anxiety and insights into thinking habits.

Centering Prayer is a spiritual practice similar to mindfulness meditation, developed by Trappist monks in the 1970s. It involves using a sacred word to symbolize surrender to God's presence and action within, helping the practitioner return to the present moment when the mind gets engaged in thoughts. Through this practice, one gains the key to inner peace: observing thoughts and nonresistance to them. This awareness provides a sense of safety and freedom, a decisive break from anxiety and endless worries. It allows for clearer thinking and creative choices.

THE BREATH OF CHRIST

TURNING ANXIETY AND WORRIES INTO PRAYER

The Jesus Prayer provides an effective way to alleviate anxiety and worries. It allows us to start exactly where we are by naming our thoughts and feelings and turning them into prayer.

Back to Sophie, who is facing a practical decision while carrying heavy loads of anxiety and distress regarding her life situation. I ask Sophie to repeat after me as I help turn her feelings and concerns into prayer.

> *Lord, I want so much to have a child of my own. Lord Jesus, help me!*
> *Lord, I am worried that my chances of having a child are running out. Lord Jesus, help me!*
> *Lord, I yearn to have my own family and to raise a child with a supportive partner. Lord Jesus, help me!*
> *Lord, I have tried so hard, but things do not turn out as I want. Lord Jesus, help me!*
> *Lord, I feel so frustrated with my life. Lord Jesus, help me!*

As she prays, she appears more settled. Sophie reports feeling calmer with each prayer as if she is unloading her burdens onto the Lord. She feels that the Lord is listening to her and sharing her burdens. She is not alone. She feels connected to Christ, who understands and cares for her. After some minutes of prayer, Sophie shares more about her life situation with me. Then Sophie stops, looks directly at me, and says, "Father, can you say more of those sentences for me?"

I am both surprised and delighted to hear her request. Sophie asks me to continue guiding her in this prayer after experiencing its fruits. She experiences the power of the Jesus Prayer, and the living Lord becomes a saving presence for her at this critical time.

Unloading Our Burdens

On this occasion, Sophie is not yet able to find an answer to her ethical dilemma, but she has found a secure base in Christ, who is accessible at all times through prayer.

RECOGNIZING ANXIETY THROUGH THE EXAMEN

Within the Ignatian tradition, the awareness examen is a powerful tool to help us recognize our anxiety and worries. As we review our day with God's loving gaze, we might notice the sweaty palms, the palpitations, and the tightness in our stomach that we have overlooked during the day. Then, we might notice the dread as we think of an approaching deadline, a social function, or a public speech. We might notice that when we are anxious, we are more irritable and impatient toward people around us. We might be more likely to drink, smoke, overeat, watch pornography, spend hours watching TV, shop, or gamble…as a way to soothe the pain of anxiety.

Once we notice anxiety, we recall that the anxious mind cannot think straight and often gets caught in useless worries. We can apply Carnegie's practical suggestions to step out of our worrying habits by living one day at a time. We might switch from worrying to problem-solving mode by asking simple questions to identify what needs to be done. However, knowing the way out of anxiety does not automatically get us out of anxiety. We need practice and a companion to get from where we are to where we need to be. The companion we need is the living Jesus, and the practice is the Jesus Prayer.

Once we gain awareness of our situation, we can turn our anxiety and worries into prayer.

Lord, I am anxious about this coming deadline. I'm not confident I can do it well or finish it on time. Lord Jesus, help me!

THE BREATH OF CHRIST

Lord, I was very irritated by my husband's behavior today. Now, I realize I was more irritable because I have been anxious about my daughter's health. Lord Jesus, help me!

Lord, when I am anxious, I feel overwhelmed and can't do any work. Lord Jesus, help me!

Lord, I often drink alcohol when I am anxious to calm myself. Lord Jesus, help me!

Lord, I want to live one day at a time, but I keep worrying about tomorrow. Lord Jesus, help me!

Lord, I often worry about what other people might think or say about me, and it makes me anxious. Lord Jesus, help me!

Lord, I keep worrying about the horrible things that could happen to my children. Lord Jesus, help me!

Lord, I need to stop worrying and attend to practical things I can do today. Lord Jesus, help me!

As we practice naming our anxiety, worries, and related behaviors, we externalize these things and turn them into prayers. As soon as we name them and turn them into prayers, we experience an easing of anxiety. As we pray, a safety zone opens up between ourselves and the threat. The Lord Jesus becomes the secure base we need in times of vulnerability and stress. We gain new insights into our current situation and can deal more constructively with our anxiety. Where once we were incapacitated by anxiety, our mind is now free to think, imagine, and be creative.

5

Healing Our Psychological Traumas

During the Spring of 2010, I was working on my thesis proposal at Boston College. It was one of the most challenging periods of my life. The constant self-doubt, criticism, and fear of failure made it hard for me to focus on my work. It felt like I was carrying a courtroom on my shoulders, with the judge, prosecutor, and executioner ready to pounce on me for every mistake I made. Every sentence I wrote was scrutinized, and every idea I had was picked apart by the inner judge.

The pressure and stress took a toll on my physical and mental health. I had frequent headaches, trouble sleeping, and a constant feeling of tightness in my gut. My desk, which used to be my sanctuary, became a place of torture. Even simple tasks felt like they lasted an eternity, while distractions like YouTube, Facebook, or emails provided temporary relief.

Later, I learned that my fears, doubts, and self-criticism were a result of my past traumas, which had been triggered by the pressures of my academic work. Seeking guidance, I visited Father Bob at the Campion Center and asked him to be my spiritual director for an eight-week retreat in daily life. Father Bob was a retired Jesuit and a skilled spiritual director, and I opted for a longer retreat to bring my struggles into prayer and develop a daily prayer practice. During the retreat, Father Bob helped me understand how past traumas could be healed with the help of a spiritual director. Moreover, I learned that the Jesus Prayer is a powerful remedy for past traumas.

UNDERSTANDING PSYCHOLOGICAL TRAUMA

Psychology tells us that many mental health issues have their roots in past experiences. Even the long-forgotten traumas from the past can cast a long shadow over our current perceptions of the world and give rise to feelings of fear, anxiety, and helplessness, even in the absence of any perceivable danger. In the spiritual journey, past traumas are also the major obstacles that hinder our growth and impair our capacity for intimacy with God. It is helpful to understand what trauma is and why it can have such a great impact on our lives.

A vast amount of research has been done in mental health and neuroscience on trauma in recent decades. However, experts in trauma research and therapy have struggled to find a definition that can account for all the complex findings and the myriad of experiences that can result from trauma. *The Encyclopedia of Psychological Trauma* offers this definition:

> A common feature of past and current definitions of psychological trauma is that it represents events that are emotionally shocking or horrifying, which threaten or actually involve death(s) or a violation of bodily integrity (such as sexual violation or torture) or that render the affected person(s) helpless to prevent or stop the resultant psychological and physical harm.[1]

I think trauma is best understood as *a painful experience that exceeds one's coping ability*. An individual can be traumatized by either physical pain or psychological pain. The International Asso-

Healing Our Psychological Traumas

ciation for the Study of Pain (IASP) defines *physical* pain as "an unpleasant sensory and emotional experience associated with, or resembling that associated with, actual or potential tissue damage."[2] In other words, physical pain is connected with a physical injury, whether actual, potential, or resembling a physical injury. The emotional component that comes in response to the unpleasant nerve signal can include apprehension, fear, anxiety, or distress.

Psychological pain refers to the experience of perceived injury to the self, to loved ones, or to persons or animals with whom we empathize. This is the experience of being betrayed, deceived, mugged, or verbally abused, where we perceive an injury to our individual self, our integrity, or our dignity as a person. A similar injury can occur when we are threatened with violence or with public humiliation—for example, by the dissemination of sensitive information or images of ourselves. We can also experience psychological pain when we witness or hear about someone we empathize with being harmed. For instance, a teacher can experience psychological pain when she hears a student telling his experiences of violence in the home. Psychological pain also has an emotional component, which can include grief, anger, fear, distress, shame, or confusion.

Psychological trauma can be defined *as an experience of pain (physical or psychological) or a perceived threat of pain that overwhelms one's coping capacity and compromises one's need for safety*. People are traumatized when they experience physical or psychological pain that is greater than what they can endure and still feel safe in the world. People can also be traumatized by the threat of death or violence to themselves or those they empathize with, where the pain they experience exceeds their coping ability. This is because each of us has a personal threshold of endurance for pain, and this threshold is related to our need for safety. If we experience pain that is below our endurance threshold, our need for safety remains intact, and in our minds, the world is safe. However, if we experience pain that exceeds our endurance threshold, our

THE BREATH OF CHRIST

need for safety is compromised, and in our minds, the world is a dangerous place.³

A traumatic event is, therefore, a terrifying event because the pain received at such magnitude tells the mind that there is a breach in the security system. Traumatized people are *fearful* people because, in their minds, the world is a treacherous place, and they cannot simply relax and go on with their lives in that unsafe environment. Note that our mind is hardwired to keep us safe. Our need for safety is the most basic of all psychological needs. It is prioritized above other needs, such as belonging, love, and esteem. According to Abraham Maslow, our mind cannot attend to those higher needs if our need for safety is compromised. But there is more to the story.

The key to understanding the devastating impact of trauma on a person is in the way the mind works to keep us safe. To help us function in the world, our mind has to generate a "world map" and a "guidebook" to provide us with knowledge about the world and how to survive in it. Our world map is a collage made of numerous pieces of mental data about places and people, along with a mental evaluation of the desirability and safety of each. Our guidebook provides directives on how to conduct ourselves and relate to other people, given the beliefs, customs, and social norms of each situation. For our world map and guidebook to serve their purposes, they have to be updated regularly with new knowledge and data from our lived experiences.

A traumatic experience is devastating because it signals to our mind that there is a breach of security. It invalidates our world map and guidebook, which are meant to keep us safe. In other words, a traumatic experience invalidates our existing version of reality: our perceptions about the world, ourselves, other people, and how to relate to them. It tells us that something is seriously wrong with the way we have perceived the world and the way we have conducted ourselves.

Traumatized persons experience a *loss of direction* because their world map and guidebook have been invalidated by the trauma.

Healing Our Psychological Traumas

They are no longer certain what to think of the world or how to conduct themselves. They are overwhelmed and paralyzed by fear about the perilous world where they no longer feel safe. The world is not safe, people are not safe, and intimacy is particularly unsafe because you are required to let down your guard and become vulnerable to another person. What if they take advantage of us? What if they hurt us? Traumatized people are often *guarded and defensive* when relating to others.

After experiencing a traumatic event, our mind tries frantically to make sense of this breach of security by scrutinizing its perceptions of reality. The search to explain the trauma can turn inward, called "internalization." Perhaps I have been too naïve to realize that the world is a treacherous place. Perhaps people are full of evil intent and are there to get me. How can I be so stupid as to trust people to keep their promises? Maybe I should not rely on my judgments and make my own decisions from now on. In short, our mind tries to explain this breach of security by laying the blame on ourselves. There must be something wrong with the way we have perceived the world, ourselves, and other people or the way we have related to them. This process of internalization of the blame can lead to *guilt, shame, self-criticism,* and a *bleaker view* of the world, of the self, and other people.

Blame can also be externalized in many cases, leading to rage, anger, or frustration against others. Very commonly, this rage and anger turns against those who are meant to keep us safe from harm: parents, teachers, older siblings and relatives, spouses, children (of older parents), or guardians. All of this is the mind's attempt to make sense of the painful experience and to keep us safe in the aftermath of a traumatic event.

Traumatic experiences vary greatly in severity, and these characteristic features also vary significantly from person to person: *fear, loss of direction, guarded and defensive behavior, a bleak view of the world,* and negative emotions such as *guilt, shame, self-criticism, frustration, rage,* and *anger.* Among these, fear is the overriding feature. It is also fear that drives the whole psychological process in response to trauma, leading to loss of direction, guardedness, a bleak view of the world, and other negative emotions.

Fortunately, the majority of people who experience trauma will recover from it. In the American Psychiatric Association's *Diagnostic and Statistical Manual of Mental Disorders, Fifth Edition*, acute stress disorder is the diagnosis of people exposed to trauma who present with symptoms within one month after exposure. Approximately half of the individuals with acute stress disorder will develop post-traumatic stress disorder (PTSD).[4] Among adults with PTSD, approximately half will recover completely within three months, while some individuals remain symptomatic for longer than twelve months or even years afterward.[5] PTSD is characterized by four general types of symptoms: unwanted memories or reminders of the trauma, attempts to avoid those memories or reminders, a reduction in the ability to feel positive emotions, and an increase in negative emotions (anger, frustration, anxiety), physical tension, sleeplessness, and watchfulness for danger.[6]

People recover from trauma when they have successfully restored their sense of security in the world and go on with their lives. This can occur in one of two ways. First, people can feel safe in the world once they have examined the nature and extent of the danger, thereby containing it and protecting themselves from it through appropriate revision of their perceptions of reality or their conduct. Second, perhaps more commonly, people can suppress the memories of the whole traumatic experience. Suppressing the memories of trauma would allow them, in the short term, to get on with life without having to continue scrutinizing their perceptions, blaming themselves or others for the trauma, and feeling fearful and lost in the world. It makes sense to suppress traumatic experiences from memory, especially when we do not have sufficient time and space, psychological tools, and support to make sense of the situation.

Suppression of traumatic memories might be helpful in the short term, and sometimes, it is the best option available at the time of trauma. But it is not the end of the story. Years later, individuals might have successfully suppressed all recollection of the painful event but continue to experience anxiety, fear, anger, or depression that has its roots in the past trauma.

This was my situation in spring 2010 when the pressures of academic work triggered in me the fears, self-doubts, self-criticism, and helplessness that were linked with my childhood traumas. Though I had no recollection of the traumas at the time, the symptoms were so severe and persistent that they obstructed my work. Over the course of the eight-week retreat, I was able to recall some traumatic experiences at school and understood how the internalization process had led to self-criticism and self-doubt. The retreat under Father Bob's guidance provided the secure base and the psychological tools I needed to unpack my past experiences. With the help of spiritual tools, including the Jesus Prayer, I was able to find healing and freedom from negative perceptions and emotions to continue with my academic work.

HEALING OF PAST TRAUMAS

Traumatized individuals often have negative feelings and outlooks about the world and people because the human mind tends to multiply and universalize the danger it cannot understand. This survival mechanism makes us afraid of situations and persons that remind us of the traumatic experience. Healing from past traumas is often a long process that involves understanding the painful event, how it has impacted one's life, and how one's need for safety is ensured at present. The individuals gain insights into how distressing the event was to them, how they have tried to cope by blaming themselves or blaming others, and how they have told themselves not to trust certain kinds of people ever again. Once they have insights into the past event and how their reaction to it has led to negative perceptions and feelings about the world, themselves, and others, there is a sense of release from the fears and negativity of the past. The world is enlarged and safe to live in, perhaps with concrete adjustments to how we perceive and relate to others. People are not all bad, and many can be trusted to keep their promises. There is freedom, lightness, and joy when healing occurs.

I have witnessed time and again the power of Christian spiritual practices, especially the efficacy of the Jesus Prayer, in healing past traumas. I believe Christianity has very powerful resources and tools for healing traumas, and when these are used appropriately, sometimes in conjunction with psychological therapy, they can help the healing process happen more rapidly and in a more wholesome manner.

Some spiritual writers have identified the accumulated pains we carry as a major obstacle in the spiritual journey. They also suggest that this burden of pain can be dissolved through spiritual practices. I shall briefly examine the works of three authors and then discuss how the Jesus Prayer can help heal traumas.

DISSOLVING PAST HURT THROUGH AWARENESS

Zen master Thich Nhat Hanh calls the accumulated pain in our psyche "internal formations," which are formed each time we feel hurt by someone's action. Because of their unpleasant nature, they are often suppressed in the subconscious, where they grow stronger and harder to deal with. Yet they can manifest in destructive thoughts, feelings, and behavior.[7]

To dissolve internal formations, we must bring them to our awareness. Negative images, thoughts, and emotions can arise and overwhelm us when we engage with these internal formations during meditation. If our consciousness is not strong enough, we will be repulsed by unpleasant feelings or become sleepy and shut

Healing Our Psychological Traumas

down. With practice, when our consciousness is strong enough, we can observe and gain insights into these emotions and the past hurts that gave rise to them, thus freeing ourselves from their control.[8]

Nhat Hanh also suggests an indirect way to dissolve internal formations. When engaging our pains, we are to embrace and soothe them with mindfulness, compassion, and love like a parent soothing a child in distress.[9] The next step is to sow the seeds of empathy and compassion daily through meditation practices and interaction with others. The seeds of compassion will weaken the internal formations over time or completely dissolve them. Once they are weakened, we can observe them with the light of awareness and transform them into positive energy.

This indirect approach is very helpful and applicable in many cases of trauma. Note Nhat Hanh's emphasis on the attitude one ought to have toward one's own pains. The right attitude toward oneself is self-compassion or self-parenting instead of self-judgment, which generates anger, fear, shame, or self-loathing each time one recalls one's painful experience. Nhat Hanh's indirect approach also points to the reality that healing from past traumas is a very complex and demanding process.

Spiritual teacher Eckhart Tolle uses the term "pain body" to describe accumulated emotional pain that becomes lodged in our mind and body. This accumulation is similar to what Nhat Hanh calls "internal formations." While the pain body is in a dormant state, certain situations can trigger it into active mode, leading to deeply negative and destructive thoughts and feelings.[10] Tolle describes the pain body as a parasitic entity that feeds on negative emotions and can overwhelm an individual with feelings of anger, hatred, grief, and destructiveness. It thrives in the absence of awareness and depends on our identification with it. To dissolve it, we must observe it and break our identification with it. By doing so, we can take away its power over us.

According to Tolle, when we identify with our pain body, we believe it is a part of who we are. This can be especially true for people who have experienced severe trauma in their past. This identification with the pain can become a significant barrier to healing. Breaking this identification means externalizing the pain or excising it from our sense of self. It is an essential first step toward healing. Like Nhat Hanh, Tolle suggests that observing the pain body with presence and acceptance is enough to bring about transformation. Once we break identification with it, the light of our awareness will weaken the pain body and eventually transmute it into energy to fuel the light of consciousness.[11]

The greatest challenge in dealing with the pain body is bringing it into consciousness. The mind has a natural aversion to the pain body because of its unpleasant nature. There is also actual danger in facing the pain body head-on because unless we have sufficient power of consciousness, we are likely to be drawn into it and re-traumatized by reliving the traumatic experiences. Each time that happens, the pain body grows, and we are left with an even stronger aversion to it. To dissolve the pain body, we must bring it into consciousness without being consumed by it. This is a great challenge that involves a contest between our consciousness and the pain body. That is why Nhat Hanh suggests that we do not face the pain body head-on but indirectly.

Thomas Keating, a Trappist monk and teacher of Centering Prayer, believes that this Christian mindfulness practice can help heal past hurts. Through what he calls the "unloading of the unconscious," emotional junk is expelled from the practitioner's mind, leading to a greater sense of well-being and inner freedom. Keating insists that through this contemplative prayer, God works within us and will reveal our wounds when we are ready for healing.[12]

In a later work, Keating terms this healing process "Divine Therapy," which involves intensifying our experience of God and allowing Him to bring emotional wounds and painful truths about ourselves to awareness both during prayer and in daily life.[13]

Keating's Centering Prayer is a spiritual practice that helps one accept and reconcile with emotional wounds. The process is gradual and can take several years. Keating maintains that the process is entirely governed by God, who knows us thoroughly and will only give us enough knowledge to handle at any given point in our spiritual journey. It is important to cultivate patience and trust in God's healing activity while avoiding the risk of being re-traumatized by examining our hurts when we are not ready.

DISSOLVING THE PAIN BODY: TURNING OUR PAIN INTO PRAYER

Back to my retreat with Father Bob in the spring of 2010. My healing journey begins when Father Bob guides me through the inner child meditation. This meditation puts me in touch with my deepest, most authentic feelings, needs, and woundedness. It also cultivates a compassionate gaze toward myself, like a caring parent looking upon a child. That gaze leads to greater patience and empathy toward myself instead of shame and self-judgment. With Jesus as my companion and Father Bob as my guide, I begin where I am: amid the overwhelming feelings of stress, doubt, and anxiety. I begin by naming these feelings and turn them into prayer.

- *Lord, I am so stressed by my work! Lord Jesus, help me!*
- *Lord, I have tried so hard, but I haven't produced anything. Lord Jesus, help me!*
- *Lord, it seems that nothing I write is ever good enough. Lord Jesus, help me!*
- *Lord, I am so anxious that I won't be able to meet the deadline. Lord Jesus, help me!*
- *Lord, I am so stressed that I can neither work nor rest. Lord Jesus, help me!*
- *Lord, I doubt whether I can ever write a thesis. Lord Jesus, help me!*

THE BREATH OF CHRIST

As soon as I do this, a new awareness comes into my situation. For the first time, I can externalize my thoughts and feelings and see them for what they are. Each time I invoke the Lord's name, I feel Jesus right next to me, listening, empathizing, and supporting me. I am no longer alone in my struggles. Once I name my stress, worries, anxiety, tiredness, and doubt and turn them into prayer, they lose their power over me. I feel lighter, as though the burden of anxiety has been contained and diminished. There is a new sense of liveliness; a new space is opening up. There is wiggle room when the anxiety and worries loosen their stranglehold on me. There is a sense of hope, of new possibilities, when I feel for myself that things are getting better. Everything in me is saying that I am getting the right remedy.

With practice, the Jesus Prayer grows deeper and deeper in me. With full presence and patience, I can see more and more deeply into my interior life and recall the childhood traumas that have continued to haunt me. I recall the experience when, as a second grader in Vietnam, I came late to school one day and was sent to the principal's office to get written permission before I could come to class. There was a teacher at the desk whom I had never seen before. He asked me for my name. When he heard my name, he asked me to say it again, then stood up and told me to wait for him there. A minute later, he came back with another teacher and asked me to say my name again. After hearing my name this time, both broke out laughing and made fun of my accent. After a few minutes of this abuse, the first teacher wrote a note for me and let me return to class.

I also recall another traumatic experience at that school. One day, some kids got caught misbehaving in class by a teacher, and they falsely blamed me for inducing them. I denied their allegation, but it was no use. I was given the straps in front of the class with the other kids.

During my retreat, these seemingly insignificant incidents rise in my awareness, and I see for the first time how they have

Healing Our Psychological Traumas

left their marks on me. In the first incident, there was the pain of a child being laughed at by the teachers and a sense of helplessness in the face of adversity. In the child's mind, there must be something wrong with his voice to explain why the teachers laughed at him. This pain was internalized, leading to shame and self-judgment. The shame began with the accent and intonation, then became generalized and extended to voice and speech. The result was truly devastating because he became ashamed of his own voice. He was ashamed to open his mouth.

In the second incident, it was the pain of the child being subjected to injustice and the sense of helplessness in his inability to defend himself against other kids' allegations. In the child's mind, the school was not safe, and other people's voices would prevail over his, though he might be right. He was confused, scared, and ashamed, so ashamed that he did not tell his parents. Again, the pain was internalized, leading to further shame, self-criticism, and helplessness.

That was thirty-six years before my retreat with Father Bob, and I have never realized these incidents had such devastating impacts on me. It was the pressure of academic work at the time that awakened my pain body from its dormant state. Subconsciously, writing the thesis proposal meant I needed to find my voice, make my case, and defend it to others. It activated the shame regarding my voice, the self-criticism, and the self-doubts that had been suppressed for over three decades.

My anxiety about the impending disaster of my thesis proposal meeting stems from childhood experiences of shame and humiliation. This supports D. W. Winnicott's insight that the catastrophe we fear may already have occurred.[14]

It was the Jesus Prayer that helped bring healing to my traumas. As I recalled the traumatic events, I talked to Jesus about what happened and asked for his saving help.

THE BREATH OF CHRIST

- *Lord, when I was in second grade, I was sent to the principal's office, and the teachers made fun of my accent. Lord Jesus, help me!*
- *Lord, I was so embarrassed when they laughed at me. I wished they would stop, but they kept making fun of me. Lord Jesus, help me!*
- *Lord Jesus, instead of blaming those teachers, I blamed myself for what happened. Lord Jesus, help me!*
- *Lord Jesus, I realize that after it happened, I became ashamed of my voice. Lord Jesus, help me!*
- *Lord, I realize that for years, I have been afraid to speak out of fear that people will laugh at my accent. Lord Jesus, help me!*
- *Lord, I have been judging myself a lot and am often dismissive of everything I write. Lord Jesus, help me!*

With the Jesus Prayer, I can face my pain, name it, and turn it into prayer. I can identify the shame and self-criticism that had stifled me and turn them into prayer. With Jesus at my side as a secure base, I can explore the traumatic experiences without being drawn into them or re-traumatized by them. Each time I name my hurt and turn it into prayer, it is brought into the light of consciousness and is transformed by grace.

With each wound being healed, it feels like I am given a new lease on life. A sense of freedom, peace, joy, and light comes with healing. Christ heals me of my traumas to the depths my eyes can see. My perceptions of the world, myself, and others are transformed with new vitality. My world is enlarged with new, exciting possibilities. The world is again a safe place to be.

In time, I also found my voice and completed my doctoral thesis. Thanks to the Jesus Prayer.

Healing Our Psychological Traumas

A FRAMEWORK FOR HEALING OF PAST TRAUMAS

While each person's healing journey is unique, I wish to name some key factors that are important for healing to take place. I hope this knowledge will be helpful for both those in search of healing and those who support them through the process.

First, it is essential to have a guide in this process, someone you can trust who can provide a reality check and support you. I have found a skilled spiritual director with sufficient knowledge and experience in trauma most helpful. Many individuals can benefit from psychotherapy. However, in some countries, therapists are bound by professional regulations not to discuss religious beliefs or practices with their clients. Perhaps in some settings, in conjunction with psychotherapy, having a spiritual director can help you access the riches of your faith tradition and monitor your progress in this healing journey.

Second, the right attitude toward your wounded self is indispensable for healing. In my case, this is provided through the inner child meditation. Healing can only occur when one can look at one's wounded self with patience, compassion, and empathy, like a loving parent looking at a child. This loving gaze must replace the shame, anger, and self-loathing that often arise as one looks at one's traumas.

Third, it is helpful to begin with your present symptoms and turn them into prayer. Start by naming your current feelings—anxiety, stress, fear, self-criticism, tiredness—and turn them into prayer by invoking Jesus's name. Trust that you will only be shown the past traumas underlying your symptoms when you are ready to deal with them.

THE BREATH OF CHRIST

Fourth, when the traumatic experiences surface, be intensely present and aware of your emotions in response to them. Then, name the traumas and your feelings and turn them into prayers. Take courage and persevere. When you first face the trauma, expect that you are likely to feel overwhelmed with dread, disgust, and shame. Name your fear or shame, and ask Jesus to help you. Take your time to pray with that fear or shame instead of running for cover. Be gentle and compassionate to yourself. If you see an experience that overwhelms you with dread, take time out, then pray with that fear. If the fear decreases after some time of prayer *and* you feel safe as you face the trauma, it means you are ready to deal with it. You can continue the process by turning that trauma and your feelings into prayer. But if the fear or shame persists with overwhelming intensity each time you face the trauma after a period of prayer, you are meant to leave it and only return to it when you are more ready.

Note that a traumatic experience you have dealt with before can surface again so that you can deal with it at a deeper level. Do not dismiss a seemingly trivial traumatic experience that comes to your mind a second time in a prayerful context. God might judge that you are ready to deal with it at a deeper level to bring about even greater healing and freedom.

Fifth, healing occurs when you can process the traumatic event and its impact, thereby containing it and ending its power over you. It comes with the acceptance that this unchangeable past event has happened to you and the choice to reject its ongoing control over your life. In each case, it requires forgiveness. First, you must forgive yourself for your behavior before, during, and after the trauma. Second, it is to forgive those who have failed to keep you safe, and the offender(s). Forgiveness is a choice to let go of a past wrong, accept that it has happened, and release all inner resentment against someone.

Once you can process the trauma, you can see with greater clarity what modifications you need to make to your world map and

Healing Our Psychological Traumas

guidebook without barring yourself from a wide range of life experiences for fear of getting hurt. The world becomes larger, safer, and brighter for you as your need for safety is met. With healing, all the psychological impacts of trauma on you are reversed. You feel inner peace, joy, freedom, and lightness. As your world expands, new possibilities open up for you. You might find creativity, laughter, humor, and spontaneity again. New friendships are conceivable as people become more trustworthy.

The Jesus Prayer is invaluable because it helps bring Jesus' healing presence to this process. The practice of naming our experiences, feelings, and thoughts and then turning them into vocal prayer serves to strengthen our awareness of what is happening inside while being grounded in our faith in Jesus. The light of our consciousness will grow brighter with this practice, thereby keeping us from being drawn into the trauma and re-traumatized. If there is a contest between our trauma and our light of consciousness, the Jesus Prayer will bolster our light of consciousness and weaken the power of trauma over us.

This, I hope, is good news for many today.

6

Turning Anger into Prayer

Andy came home tired and hungry after a stressful day at work. He saw his wife Josie in the kitchen and said, "This house is a mess!" As Josie heard the tone of admonition in his voice, she felt a wave of anger well up inside. It grew stronger as she remembered how busy she had been after she left work early to pick up their sick daughter Emmy from school and attend to her. The anger became a raging storm as she realized that Andy was referring to the mess he and his friends had left behind after a social night....

UNDERSTANDING ANGER

This hypothetical scenario illustrates several key aspects of anger. It is an emotional response to the hurt, threat, or injustice we experience. It has cognitive, physical, and behavioral components. Cognitively, Josie perceives Andy's statement as an admonition, and she judges this admonition as hurtful and unjust. Biologically, her limbic system evaluates the verbal input as a threat and triggers a neurological response through the amygdala, resulting in physical arousal with increased heart rate, rapid breathing, and increased blood flow to the muscles. Josie is physically aroused for vigorous action in response to the threat.

Turning Anger into Prayer

This anger response has an evolutionary advantage in helping us protect ourselves from threats and dangers. In her influential work, Harriet Lerner wrote, "Our anger may be a message that we are being hurt, that our rights are being violated, that our needs or wants are not being adequately met, or simply that something is not right."[1]

Aaron Karmin, a specialist in anger management for men, believes that anger is a secondary feeling: people feel angry in response to another feeling, such as fear, hopelessness, hurt, disappointment, or guilt.[2] These feelings are connected with vulnerability, and many men use anger to cover up or protect themselves from this feeling of vulnerability or emotional pain. Underlying anger are the needs for safety, empathy, trust, respect, support, affirmation, autonomy, and so on. When people listen to their anger and attend to the underlying needs, its intensity subsides.[3]

THE HIGH COSTS OF ANGER

Contrary to the common idea that expressing anger is normal and healthy, research has shown that anger (either expressed or unexpressed) increases the risks of hypertension, heart disease, and gastric ulcers.[4] Apart from these physical costs, angry people often find themselves dissatisfied and helpless. This is because when they use anger to express their needs, such as the need for assistance, nurturance, safety, empathy, or support, they push people away, thereby diminishing the chances of getting what they need. Constant anger does not help fulfill one's needs. In reality, it leads others to become defensive and distance themselves. With every angry outburst, the individual feels more helpless because they are less able to get what they need from others. This leads to isolation and loneliness when the individual feels distant and disconnected from others.[5] When anger is the default reaction to life occurrences over time, it becomes a harmful habit.[6]

THE BREATH OF CHRIST

In addition to these personal costs, expressed anger can damage relationships with friends, work colleagues, one's spouse, or one's children. When you frequently become angry, it damages your relationships by diminishing others' goodwill, appreciation, and care toward you. People perceive angry individuals as dangerous and handle them with caution or avoid them entirely. Although anger can initially be effective in stopping unwanted behavior, it can ultimately lead to emotional distancing. People become vigilant and guarded when you are around. The more anger you express, the less you are listened to and the more isolated you become.[7]

Anger can easily lead to a vicious cycle of aggression and hostility. The more we act aggressively, the angrier we become as anger gains momentum and takes over our thinking and behavior.[8] Frequent expressions of anger can harm relationships by reducing tolerance, flexibility, and empathy. Using anger to control others may get us the results we want immediately, but not for long. People quickly develop strategies to counter rage through avoidance or passive aggression.[9]

Anger can be adaptive when it helps us establish and maintain appropriate boundaries, assert our needs, and protect our integrity. It provides the energy we need to respond to emotional or physical threats. However, it is important to channel this energy through assertiveness instead of hostility or aggression to bring about positive changes. Anger tells us something is wrong and motivates us to address it. But anger in itself does not usually get us what we want. It is how we act that influences the way people respond to us.

VENTILATION DOES NOT REDUCE ANGER

In the 1960s and 1970s, it was widely believed that ventilation was a healthy way to deal with anger,[10] but research has disproved this view. This ventilationist view is based on the idea that anger is a kind of energy that builds up inside a person, and unless it is released, that energy can damage the person's mental and physical health. Suppressed anger is thought to be the root cause of problems such as sadness, lethargy, depression, high blood pressure, and heart problems. It was believed that ventilating anger would reduce this buildup of bad energy and the health problems it causes. However, experimental studies have consistently shown that venting anger does not reduce anger. It simply reinforces an angry attitude and can make people angrier.[11] Expressing anger by yelling, hitting, or breaking things does not alleviate anger but increases it. Research has shown that, instead of providing relief and health benefits, venting anger leads to more anger, tension, and arousal.[12]

VENTING ANGER ON THE INNOCENT

In the Vietnamese language, there is a popular idiom, "*Giận cá chém thớt,*" which literally means to chop (*chém*) a wooden cutting board (*thớt*) instead of the fish (*cá*) that caused anger (*giận*). This is when someone directs their anger toward another person who is not responsible for the situation. For example, a man may be angry with his boss at work, but instead of confronting his boss, he goes home and takes out his anger on his wife. In Freud's psychoanalysis, this is known as displacement, a defense mechanism that involves redirecting anger from its original source to a safer or more socially acceptable target. This mechanism helps individuals manage their negative emotions and avoid direct confrontation with the original cause of their distress.[13]

In her influential work, Carol Tavris reviews the research literature on anger and emphasizes that anger is a choice. According to her, judgment and choice differentiate human beings from other

THE BREATH OF CHRIST

species and are the hallmarks of human anger.[14] Matthew McKay and his coauthors similarly argue that individuals *choose* to be angry.[15] In other words, people have control over their expression of anger, including whether to direct it toward a specific person in a certain situation. Tavris also points out that anger serves as a form of policing, using its forceful nature and threat of retaliation to maintain order in situations such as family conflicts, disputes with neighbors, or disagreements in business where official law is not practical, unsuitable, or unavailable.[16]

Anger can only serve a judicial function in relationships where retaliation is possible. It can keep people's behavior in check and enforce fair play, but only if angry outbursts can be met with equally forceful counterattacks or other forms of social penalty. Unfortunately, retaliation is often not an option in relationships where there is a power discrepancy between the parties. If a man with more power feels little threat of retaliation or penalty, he is less hesitant about taking out his anger on someone with less power. Sadly, in patriarchal societies such as Vietnam and the Philippines, men often redirect their anger toward their wives and children without fear of retaliation or social penalty. Over time, angry outbursts might become a regular habit, and they might blame their family for their anger or claim they have no control over their actions. This claim is merely an excuse to take it out on their family.

If anger is a choice, why do men choose to vent their anger on those closest to them? Because it is safe for them to do so. Where there is no fear of retaliation or penalty, people choose anger because it gets them what they want. It cultivates fear in others and gives them power and control over household members. As McKay and his coauthors point out, using anger to manipulate others can work for a short time, but people will quickly develop effective ways to protect themselves. The habit of venting anger on the innocent is not an uncontrollable primal instinct but a tool to manipulate and control others.

THE TWO-STEP MODEL: THE FUEL OF ANGER AND WHAT IGNITES IT

McKay and his coauthors propose a two-step model in which stress has a key role in the anger response. They identify stress as the fuel of anger and "trigger thoughts" as the sparks that set it aflame. Anger is a two-step process. The first step is the experience of stress and the motivation to cope with it. The second is the activation of trigger thoughts that convert stress into anger. These trigger thoughts come in the form of "blamers" and "shoulds."[17] A "blamer" accuses someone of intentionally causing you harm through their wrongful behavior. A "should" statement suggests that the other person is aware of what is right but chooses to ignore it due to their own selfishness or lack of consideration.

These two types of trigger thoughts arise from the belief that the other person is to blame or has bad intentions and, therefore, should be corrected or penalized. These trigger statements evoke anger because they portray oneself as a victim of someone else's wrongdoing. By blaming others, people can avoid taking responsibility for their unhappy situation. Once anger is triggered, it generates more arousal and often more trigger thoughts, which then feed into the anger cycle.

This two-step model provides a corrective for the ventilationist view. It is not anger that accumulates but stress from physical or emotional pain, frustration, and threats. Anger is only one of many ways to cope with stress. As McKay and his coauthors point out, there are effective and less harmful ways to reduce stress, such as crying, exercising, humor, relaxation, verbalizing pain, recreation, problem-solving, music, and resting.[18]

THE BREATH OF CHRIST

PRINCIPLES OF ANGER MANAGEMENT

From their two-step model, McKay and coauthors propose a helpful approach to anger management. By recognizing stress as its root cause and the thought patterns that trigger it, we can make conscious decisions to reduce the likelihood of angry outbursts. According to the authors, anger management consists of (1) combating trigger thoughts and (2) reducing stress. Being mindful of our thoughts can help us manage our anger. By tuning in to our physical and mental states, we can recognize stress and deal with it before something sets it aflame and turns it into anger. We have the power to choose how we feel.[19]

The crucial step in anger management is to take responsibility for our anger.

To combat the fallacious assumptions behind trigger thoughts, the authors explain that no one knows and understands our needs better than we do. It is appropriate for others to prioritize their own needs as well. Conflicts over needs are bound to happen between people. Our satisfaction in life is determined by how well we can meet our needs and avoid pain.[20]

Instead of blaming others, we need to take responsibility for our pain and recognize that we must adapt our strategies in order to better fulfill our needs.[21] Taking responsibility can help us find more effective ways to meet our needs. It is helpful to recognize common situations when we feel frustrated in relationships and take positive action. We can change our behavior rather than expect others to change theirs to meet our needs. For example, if we want to spend more quality time with someone, we can use incentives or plan enjoyable activities together instead of blaming them for not wanting to spend time with us. Alternatively, we tend to our own needs if that helps reduce our stress levels. We can also go elsewhere to fulfill our need for connection, support, and nourishment rather than continuing to demand one particular person

Turning Anger into Prayer

give us what we need. We can set limits by saying no when necessary and being assertive in asking for what we need. Taking care of ourselves and avoiding exhaustion can also help reduce stress.[22]

TAKING TIME OUT

Taking time-out when we start feeling angry is the first step in anger management. It helps limit the harm we can cause ourselves and others if things get out of hand. The objective of time-out is to calm down from the heat of anger. Practical steps such as mindful breathing, closing our eyes, taking a walk, and drinking a cool, nonalcoholic beverage might be helpful in reducing our heart rate and calming our minds.

Once we are calm enough, if we watch what is going on in our minds, we can catch the trigger thoughts. In the scenario above, Josie needs time-out to process what is going on. If she tunes in to her feelings and thoughts, Josie might notice how stressed she has been since she heard about her daughter's condition and left work to pick her up from school. This stress turned into anger when she heard Andy's comment. Paying attention to her thoughts, Josie might notice what she is saying to herself. For example, *This is outrageous! Does he have any idea what I have been doing all day? Does he care enough to ask how I am? Is he blaming me for the mess he and his mates made? Does he expect me to clean up after him? I won't take it anymore. Who does he think he is?*

Zen master Thich Nhat Hanh uses the analogy of a mother soothing her crying child to describe taking time-out to cool the flame of anger. He compares anger to a child in distress that needs a mother's soothing embrace. We need to embrace our anger while practicing mindful breathing so that the light of mindfulness might enter and allow us to observe our anger and what has set it aflame.[23] When we embrace our anger with a lot of tenderness, we feel immediate relief and gain insight into the situation.

McKay and his coauthors suggest that after taking time-out and checking in with ourselves, we choose the opposite approach. This involves smiling, relaxing our muscles, speaking in a calm and measured tone, disengaging from the situation, resolving to address it at a later time, or expressing empathy instead of attacking.[24]

REDUCE STRESS, REDUCE ANGER

The two-step model helpfully suggests that reducing stress is the key to long-term anger management. As stress is a universal phenomenon, it is important to find stress-reduction strategies that work for us. Many people find resting, recreation, music, humor, physical exercises, and relaxation effective for reducing stress. Mindfulness exercises and yoga practice have proved helpful for many practitioners.

Problem-solving is an essential part of long-term stress reduction. Problem-solving is what we do to fulfill our needs, which may require seeking assistance or cooperation from others. The key to success is effective communication. Rather than staying silent and ignoring our needs out of fear of upsetting others or being overly aggressive to get what we want, we can express our feelings and needs while still respecting the rights of others.[25] It is possible to emphasize what we need while protecting ourselves and avoiding blame. It is also possible to set boundaries without alienating others. Assertive communication is effective for various interpersonal issues, including those related to money, power dynamics, and conflicts at home and in the workplace. The essential components of assertive communication are being straightforward, clear, and nonconfrontational.

On anger management, Karmin also highlights the significance of self-care, increasing our tolerance for frustration, and maintaining a positive outlook.[26] Practicing self-care is an essential step toward managing anger, as our feelings of vulnerability often stem from a need for safety and care. Karmin believes forgiveness is a powerful remedy for frustration, as it involves learning to let go of painful emotions associated with certain individuals or events. Maintaining a positive outlook allows us to entertain alternative interpretations of events and people's behavior without getting bogged down by negative emotions and judgments.

TURNING ANGER INTO PRAYER

Each time we are triggered, taking time-out is the key to successfully handling our anger. When we take time-out, we create the space we need to process the situation and check in with ourselves. This crucial step can save us a lot of hurt and regret. Once we take time-out, praying the Jesus Prayer is a very effective way to soothe our anger and gain insight into the situation. We can start by naming our feelings and thoughts and turning them into prayers.

In the case scenario above, Josie can begin by expressing her emotions to Jesus, then articulating her thoughts and turning them into prayers. For example:

- *Lord, this is outrageous! I am so angry! Lord Jesus, help me!*
- *Lord, I am so stressed and tired! Lord Jesus, help me!*
- *Lord, does he have any idea what I have been doing all day? Lord Jesus, help me!*
- *Lord, is he blaming me for the mess he and his mates made? Lord Jesus, help me!*
- *Lord, does he expect me to clean up after him? Lord Jesus, help me!*
- *Lord, I won't take it anymore. Who does he think he is? Lord Jesus, help me!*

THE BREATH OF CHRIST

As soon as we name our raging emotions and thoughts and turn them into prayer, we feel relief from their grips and the return to peace and calm. A space opens up with the Lord where we feel safe, understood, supported, and cared for. Like a child in distress finding the soothing embrace of the mother, we discover that our anger loses its intensity when we turn to the Lord Jesus for help. Naming our anger in this prayerful space creates a distance between ourselves and the anger. It breaks our identification with anger. It makes anger something external to us. In doing so, we break the anger cycle by disrupting the feedback loop between thoughts and emotions. When we observe anger as something "out there," it loses its intensity. After a few minutes of focused prayer, we have the calmness we need to engage in problem-solving.

To practice assertive communication, Josie needs to inform Andy about Emmy, seek his help, and remind him to clean up after himself. It is impossible when angry to say these things without attacking the other. We need to put out the flame before we can practice assertive communication. That is why taking time-out and turning to Jesus in prayer is so crucial before we engage in problem-solving and communication to get the help we need.

* *Lord, I must tell him about Emmy. But I am so angry right now. Lord Jesus, help me!*
* *Lord, I need his help. I am so upset I don't want to talk to him. Lord Jesus, help me!*
* *Lord, I need to tell him it's his responsibility to clean up after himself. Lord Jesus, help me!*

Once she finds the calmness she needs, Josie can tell Andy things such as, "*Emmy is not well. I had to pick her up from school and take her to the doctor's today.…Could you check on her and then set the table, please? After dinner, I can help you clean up the lounge.…*"

Turning Anger into Prayer

The Jesus Prayer is a powerful tool for quelling anger and overcoming trigger thoughts. It enables us to think clearly and seek help without resorting to blame or hostility.

The Jesus Prayer can be very helpful when we feel angry due to violated boundaries or harm to our sense of self. It can assist in processing our feelings and needs and determining a reasonable response. For example, if a boss demands too much from us, the prayer can help us overcome anger and fear and provide the calmness and courage we need to practice assertive communication.

Practicing the Jesus Prayer over time can also reduce the likelihood of feeling angry by decreasing stress and frustration, which are primary drivers of anger. When we experience frustration from unfulfilled needs for support or companionship and are tempted to blame others, the prayer can help dissolve negative emotions and thoughts.

- *Lord, I had traveled three hours to spend the weekend with my friend, but she only wanted me to help her with her family issues. I am tired and angry. Lord Jesus, help me!*
- *Lord, I had hoped to get some rest last weekend with my friend but didn't get any. I am angry because I think it was her fault. Lord Jesus, help me!*
- *Lord, I have been upset with my friend, but now I realize that she has her own needs and priorities as well. Lord Jesus, help me!*
- *Lord, perhaps I shouldn't blame my friend and look instead for other ways to get some rest. Lord Jesus, help me!*

The Jesus Prayer offers a safe space for us to process our overwhelming emotions. It helps soothe our anger and provides the calm we need to work through our thoughts and find our unmet

THE BREATH OF CHRIST

needs. It also brings insight and calmness to our inner storm, extinguishing the flame of anger. This prayer helps us to engage in problem-solving and gives us the courage and composure to communicate effectively with others, thereby getting the help we need or finding other ways to fulfill our needs.

7
Counteracting Negative Self-Talk

Anna is a mother of two adult children. She possesses remarkable intelligence, organization, and communication skills, which makes her highly effective in her role as a coordinator of a mental health service. In addition, she is enrolled as a part-time student in a spirituality program, which she really enjoys. However, whenever she has to write an essay, she feels helpless and stressed, and as a result she procrastinates. Although she has a good grasp of the subject matter, she struggles to complete the task on time. Anna has made significant progress in dealing with her past hurts through her study and personal work in psychology and spirituality. However, whenever she sits down to write, she is debilitated by the thought that she can't do it. She stares at the computer screen for hours, feeling discouraged and confused. As the deadline approaches, she becomes increasingly stressed by the pressure to complete the task and her nagging doubt about her ability.

Anna's experience highlights a common phenomenon that often evades our attention—negative thoughts that automatically arise in our minds. Even the most intelligent, articulate, and competent individuals can become incapacitated by a stream of self-criticism and lose confidence in their abilities. This can result in procrastination and more stress as deadlines approach. Many of us avoid situations where we might experience rejection or disapproval, while others are deeply affected by people's criticism, feeling as though the world is ending. This chapter discusses how negative self-talk can harm our self-esteem, undermine our confidence, and prevent us from living happy and fulfilling lives. It also provides a solution to counteract its impact by using the Jesus Prayer.

THE INNER CRITIC AND NEGATIVE SELF-TALK

In cognitive behavioral therapy, automatic negative thoughts (ANTs) are negative thoughts that appear in our minds spontaneously and often without conscious effort. Negative self-talk is a type of ANT that involves negative thoughts about ourselves, our abilities, and our worth. ANTs can lead to psychological problems such as depression and anxiety disorders. Identifying and naming our inner critic can help manage negative self-talk and separate these thoughts from who we are.

In the story above, whenever Anna sits down to write an essay, her mind is filled with automatic negative thoughts, making her anxious and stressed. By observing her thoughts, Anna will notice how her inner critic convinces her of her inability to write and discourages her from trying to avoid failure. Understanding and naming her inner critic gives Anna the power to disarm it, freeing herself from its control.

Living with the critic is like being trapped in a never-ending trial where you are constantly judged and criticized for everything you do. The critic has you believe you are worthless and need to prove your worth through your achievements. This belief is behind your drive for perfectionism and constant craving for approval. In the critic's courtroom, you are a screw-up if you are not perfect. If you are not the best, you are nothing or a loser. Even the slightest mistake is used to convince you that something is wrong with you. The critic punishes you for your failures but never acknowledges your efforts or accomplishments. It compares you to others to put

Counteracting Negative Self-Talk

you down and make you try even harder. The critic blames you when things go wrong and calls you stupid, incompetent, selfish, weak, lazy, or an idiot without the slightest hesitation.

The problem is that we believe our critic, thinking everything it says about us is true and accurate. Self-criticism can be insidious, as it often aligns with the messages we were told in childhood. We tend to accept these criticisms without questioning them. With each attack, the critic chips away at our confidence, robs us of the joy of living, and fills us with self-doubt and anxiety. Eventually, this can lead to low self-esteem and self-loathing, resulting in psychological problems such as depression, anxiety disorders, self-harm, and suicidal thoughts.

To repudiate the critic and free ourselves from its courtroom requires that we understand its origin, function, and the tactics it uses to keep us in bondage. We can learn to neutralize its attacks and make it useless by finding healthier ways to fulfill our needs without it. This will allow us to move forward with confidence, knowing that our self-worth is not tied to personal achievements but rather rooted in God's love and mediated by our own self-compassion.

THE ORIGIN AND FUNCTION OF THE CRITIC

According to McKay and Fanning, our inner critic is developed in childhood as our parents enforce discipline on us.[1] Positive gestures like smiling, praising, hugging, and kissing are used to encourage good behavior, while negative gestures such as frowning, scolding, and punishing are used to discourage bad behavior. As children, we depend on our parents for protection and nourishment, so negative gestures from parents are very threatening because we fear losing their support. This is why parental disapproval feels like a major threat to our survival.

THE BREATH OF CHRIST

With the emerging sense of self during childhood, we also develop a sense of self-worth based on how our parents relate to us. When our parents consistently show us love, care, and attention, we feel valuable and deserving of affection. However, if our parents are inconsistent with their discipline or if they frequently use negative gestures, we tend to develop a negative perception of our self-worth. If parents often use words like "lazy," "selfish," "screw-up," or "bad" to express disapproval, children may feel that they are inherently bad or unworthy. As they grow up, children start to associate their parents' disapproval with a sense of personal inadequacy. Disapproving gestures are especially damaging to a child's self-worth when they are tied to anger or withdrawal of support.[2] These negative experiences from childhood can leave emotional residues that most people carry into adulthood. The critic's voice often carries the weight of parental disapproval and evokes the fear of rejection from childhood. That is why it often sounds so intimidating and disempowering.

According to Shirzad Chamine, the critic or judge, along with its accomplices, originally had a crucial role when we were children: it helped us survive our childhood.[3] Our judge develops unique characteristics in response to our survival needs in childhood. It helps us create a mental construct to explain our experiences, but its interpretation is often flawed and biased. Nonetheless, it is useful in early life to sort out who we are and how the world around us works.[4] As we grow older, such survival strategies become obsolete and need to be replaced with more appropriate tools for adulthood. In other words, although our inner critic was once helpful in our survival, it is no longer beneficial or necessary in our adult life. To use an employment metaphor, our critic's job description is outdated, its work contract has expired, its performance record is appalling, and it has cost us too much in terms of physical and mental health, life opportunities, and personal relationships. Despite this, we have not dismissed it because we have not evaluated it. It is time to let it go and replace it with more constructive approaches.

As noted by McKay and Fanning, our inner critic is constantly active because we unknowingly reinforce it by listening to its voice. The critic is reinforced because it helps us satisfy some of our basic needs, even though the cost is usually very high. It is crucial to comprehend the critic's function and purpose so as to render it redundant.

The critic motivates us to do the right thing by following rules and warns us about consequences. It can also be overly harsh and judgmental. It often enforces unrealistic and inflexible rules, causing guilt and shame when we break them. The critic can motivate us to achieve success, but it often sets unattainable standards and reinforces them with self-punishment and comparison with others. This type of motivation can be very damaging to physical and mental health in the long term.

The critic often damages our self-esteem, but it also motivates us to strive for perfection. This drive can sometimes lead to great results and a temporary boost in self-esteem, which then motivates us to keep listening to the critic. Individuals with low self-esteem rely heavily on their inner critic to cope with anxiety, fear, and inadequacy. The critic helps them feel safe in the world by avoiding risks and social interactions. However, this coping mechanism can further damage their self-esteem and lead to self-directed anger.[5]

These are the reasons we reinforce the inner critic despite the harm it causes. Understanding this helps counteract its attacks and make it redundant.

IS THE INNER CRITIC THE BAD SPIRIT?

As we examine the detrimental effects of the inner critic on our mental health, it is worth considering whether it is the same as the bad spirit in Ignatian spirituality. At the conceptual level, it is easy to see that the inner critic and the bad spirit are two distinct entities. While the inner critic is a psychological mechanism developed during childhood that persists into adult life, the bad spirit (in the narrow sense) is the spiritual entity that leads us away from God and brings desolation to our souls. However, in practice, the diabolical spiritual entity can use the inner critic to disturb our souls, obstruct our spiritual growth, and lead us away from God.

According to McKay and Fanning, the inner critic is a psychological mechanism that helps us survive childhood but becomes redundant in adult life.[6] Yet in severe cases, it can lead a person to self-harm or even suicide. It is difficult to explain in psychological terms how a mechanism that once helped us survive can turn against us in such a destructive way. I believe that in such cases, the inner critic becomes a tool for the diabolical spirit to affect the soul.

In his Spiritual Exercises, St. Ignatius points out that people can experience interior movements caused by both good and bad spirits. While the good spirit leads us toward God, the bad spirit draws us into sin or otherwise obstructs our path to God. In the Rules for Discernment, St. Ignatius refers to *the enemy*, the *enemy of human nature*, the *evil spirit*, the *bad spirit*, and the *evil Angel* with *damnable intention*, *great malice*, *wickedness*, *deceit*, and *perverse intentions* (314–35).[7] According to St. Ignatius, though the bad spirit might appear under different guises, its ultimate intention is contrary to human flourishing.

Jesuit scholar Jules Toner explains that for Ignatius, the term "spirits" in the context of "discernment of spirits" refers to the Holy Spirit and angels on one side and Satan and demons on the other.[8] Toner maintains that the term "evil spirits" should be understood in a broader sense, which includes not only Satan and demons but also our egoistic and disordered tendencies, as well as the evil influence of other individuals or society. Drawing from Toner's view, Timothy Gallagher proposes that the term "evil spirit" or

Counteracting Negative Self-Talk

"enemy" can encompass three things: (1) Satan and demons, (2) the weakness in our human nature, or the flesh (Gal 5:17), and (3) the malign influence in our society and culture.[9]

The inner critic is a psychological mechanism distinct from the bad spirit in the narrow sense. In other words, it is not the voice of Satan or any demon. However, if we use the term "bad spirit" in a broader sense, the inner critic can sometimes be categorized as such, but not always. For instance, when the inner critic motivates us to do the right thing, it does not fall under the category of a bad spirit. However, when it leads us to despair, self-loathing, and self-harm, the inner critic could be considered a bad spirit. In simpler terms, the bad spirit can use the inner critic for its wicked end.

THE CRITIC'S TACTICS: COGNITIVE DISTORTIONS

Cognitive distortions are negative thinking patterns that people use to interpret reality. They are the critic's tactics to undermine self-worth and keep people under control. Understanding these tactics will help people neutralize the critic's attacks and free themselves from its tyrannical rule. The following are common forms of cognitive distortions.[10]

Overgeneralization refers to the tendency to make a sweeping judgment about one's overall character or future possibilities based on one piece of data or experience. It harms our self-confidence and discourages us from trying new things. You can recognize overgeneralization when absolute terms like "never," "always," "all," "every," "no one," "nobody," or "everyone" are used.[11] It is important to recognize these overgeneralizations and work against them by using accurate language.

Global labeling is a type of overgeneralization in which harmful labels are used. These labels are typically derogatory terms such as

THE BREATH OF CHRIST

"failure," "gutless," "screw-up," "hopeless," "stupid," "useless," "selfish," "hypocrite," and "worthless."[12] They can be highly demoralizing and discouraging, as they carry emotional baggage from past experiences and stifle learning and growth. Such labels are unfair and highly inaccurate, and nobody should ever be subjected to them.[13]

Filtering is a harmful habit that focuses only on negative aspects while ignoring the positive and life-affirming ones. It's like a detective searching for evidence to prove you are incompetent, ugly, or worthless. This filtering process is dangerous to your self-esteem and mental health. It deletes joy and gratitude from your life.

All-or-nothing thinking is a harmful pattern of thinking in which you are judged based on extreme categories of all or nothing, good or bad, or black or white. It sets impossible standards for you to achieve and fails to acknowledge that growth and self-improvement come from making mistakes and learning from them. This pattern is the foundation for perfectionism and performance anxiety, leading to stress and exhaustion.[14]

Self-blame is a common tendency of your inner critic to hold you responsible for everything, even if you are not at fault. It blames you for your imperfections and also for things that are partially beyond your control, such as your poor health or your adult children's financial losses.[15] Self-blame can also be a way to cope with your anger toward someone you love or admire by turning it inward and attacking yourself. This can severely damage self-esteem and lead to negative long-term consequences.[16]

Personalization is the tendency to think everything, especially if it is unpleasant, has to do with you. You take everyone's complaint as directed against you. You take your wife's complaint about your son's trouble at school as a complaint against you for not being a good father. As David Burns points out, this distortion is the mother of guilt because you assume responsibility for a negative event when there is no basis at all.[17]

Paranoid mind reading occurs when you assume that everyone

Counteracting Negative Self-Talk

shares your negative views about yourself. This thinking pattern is harmful because it amplifies the inner critic's grip on you. It's important to remember that people have their own thoughts and opinions, and the only way to know for sure what someone is thinking is to ask them directly.

Control fallacies are distorted beliefs that you either have control over everything or no control over anything in life. Those with overcontrol distortion would feel personally responsible for ensuring people around them do the right thing and that things happen in the right way. On the other hand, those who have undercontrol distortion believe that they have no control over their life circumstances or the actions of others. They feel like helpless victims and are constantly berated by their inner critic, which tells them they are weak, helpless, and unable to effect change.

Emotional reasoning is a pattern of thinking that involves making conclusions based on how we feel. It is a prevalent feature of depression, where people tend to feel negative about things and assume that they are. One of the common traps of emotional thinking is procrastination, which arises when you are not in the mood to do a task and think it is impossible to complete. To avoid making false assumptions, it is essential to recognize emotional reasoning and counter it with logical thinking.

Understanding these cognitive distortions will help us neutralize the critic's attacks.

HOW TO CATCH THE INNER CRITIC

In order to counteract the critical voice in our heads, we must first become aware of it. This voice can be heard amid the constant stream of thought throughout the day as we interpret experiences, solve problems, engage with people, or consider the future. By paying attention to this internal monologue, we can recognize when the critic is speaking. The critic might say things like "You're hopeless," "What a stupid thing to say," "You're embarrassing yourself," or "You're so boring." It might compare us to others to make us feel inferior. It might bring up images of our past mistakes or failures to chastise us.[18]

McKay and Fanning suggest that we try to catch the critic especially when we are in problematic situations such as meeting strangers, contact with people we find sexually attractive, situations where we have made a mistake, interacting with an authority figure, or situations where we risk rejection, failure, or disapproval.[19] The authors propose that we devote three days to observing our inner critic, initially counting the number of negative statements he makes in a day and subsequently recording them in a notebook.

When we examine the critic's attacks, there are some common patterns that can be identified in the types of attacks received. These attacks are often highly repetitive and based on distorted assumptions about who we are and how we should behave. They usually assume that we are worthless and must prove ourselves worthy of acceptance and belonging through our achievements. This can often drive us toward higher levels of achievement or self-improvement. However, it can also invalidate who we are and what we do with an arsenal of "shoulds" and words like "lazy," "stupid," "idiot," "screw-up," or "hopeless." These criticisms often hold us to perfectionistic standards and do not tolerate failures or mistakes. This lack of empathy and compassion means that the critic's drive can be relentless, leading to exhaustion and burnout. These types of attacks are often related to the fear of rejection, disapproval, or failure.

Understanding these traits can help us recognize when the critic is active. The inner critic is driven by the need for survival, and it operates by leveraging fear of rejection and the promise of approval as motivators. This drive is persistent and unyielding, constantly pushing us to strive for perfection and avoid failure.

Counteracting Negative Self-Talk

According to McKay and Fanning, one way to identify the inner critic is by examining our self-evaluation in the areas we consider important.[20] They note that we often use negative and inaccurate language to describe our weaknesses, and these words might be the same ones used by the inner critic. For example, if someone values intellectual capabilities and achievements, the inner critic might attack them using words like "stupid," "screw-up," "idiot," "incompetent," and "imposter." If someone else values personal appearance, the critic might use words like "buck teeth," "big nose," "flat chest," and "fat thighs" in its attacks.

In his bestselling self-help book on depression, *Feeling Good*, David Burns highlights that being overly sensitive to criticism can be a sign of low self-esteem. People with this trait often react strongly to criticism because of certain assumptions they hold. These assumptions include believing that if someone criticizes them, it must be true, that their worth is based on their achievements, and that one mistake can ruin everything, making them a failure. They also think that people will not accept their imperfections and that they have to be perfect to earn respect and affection. When they make a mistake, they will face severe disapproval and punishment, which will make them feel worthless.[21]

Once these assumptions are exposed, it becomes clear just how absurd they are, and it becomes easier to dismiss them. Understanding these assumptions can help us stop beating ourselves up each time we are criticized by others.

The awareness examen in Ignatian spirituality is a helpful tool for catching the inner critic. We can tell the critic is at work when we detect the disturbance it typically causes, the words and tone it uses, and the drive to achieve, the perfectionistic standards, the concerns about one's unworthiness, the comparison with others, the shame about one's appearance or voice, the fear of rejection, or concerns about belonging it initiates in us.

Journaling is also a useful tool to recognize the patterns of thoughts that arise over time, especially during difficult times. Tuning in to what we often tell ourselves in difficult times will help us identify the critic's voice and the hidden assumptions behind its attacks. It can also be beneficial to have an experienced counselor or spiritual director who can help us identify the attack patterns of our inner critic.

HOW TO DISARM THE INNER CRITIC

Once we understand the critic's origin, function, and tactics, we can disarm and dismiss it. The cognitive behavioral therapy approach to counteracting negative self-talk is to build up self-esteem through accurate self-assessment using the self-concept inventory or similar tools. By avoiding pejorative language and overgeneralizing negatives, we can rewrite our self-evaluation and achieve a healthier sense of self, reducing the intensity of self-criticism.[22] It is also important to establish a positive inner voice that can counteract the inner critic during moments of self-doubt. This involves adopting a compassionate attitude toward ourselves, which includes self-acceptance, understanding, and forgiveness. Instead of constantly judging and comparing, we can practice compassion and cultivate a nonjudgmental attitude toward ourselves and others.[23]

Talking back can be a powerful and satisfying way to disarm our inner critic, especially when we respond with the same tone and intensity that it uses against us. Talking back has two major benefits. First, it empowers us to challenge the critic's authority. Our inner critic often sounds so formidable because he carries the authority of a disciplining parent. By talking back, we question the critic's authority and reclaim our power. Second, talking back allows us to expose the erroneous assumptions behind the critic's attacks. When we expose the critic's fallibility, it loses power over us.

Counteracting Negative Self-Talk

TELLING JESUS ABOUT THE INNER CRITIC

Once we tune into our thoughts and emotions, either in real time or in retrospection, we can identify the inner critic's voice and the inner turmoil it causes. The Ignatian spiritual practice of awareness examen is particularly helpful in reviewing areas where we tend to be self-critical. This daily practice enables us to focus on our inner world and recognize the patterns of disturbance, identifying the inner critic by the effects it has on us. We can then turn to Jesus and tell him about our inner critic. For example, in Anna's struggle with essay writing, the conversation can begin like this,

* *Lord, each time I sit down at the computer, my critic says I can't do it. Lord Jesus, help me!*
* *Lord, my critic tries to protect me from the fear of failure by discouraging me from trying. I believe it, and I am frozen with fear and self-doubt. Lord Jesus, help me!*
* *Lord, I fear that if I write an awful paper, people will be disappointed in me and judge me. Lord Jesus, help me!*
* *Lord, I fear that people will know how bad and incapable I am, and they won't respect me. Lord Jesus, help me!*
* *Lord, deep down, I believe that I must earn people's respect and love through my achievements. Otherwise, they will reject me. Lord Jesus, help me!*
* *Lord, if people reject me, I will be lonely and miserable. Lord Jesus, help me!*

Speaking with the Lord in this context helps us become more aware of the critic's voice, its intention, and how it affects our thoughts and emotions. By turning to the Lord Jesus, we can process our feelings and gain new perspectives. Verbalizing the critic's words helps us separate ourselves from the negative self-talk and take control of our thoughts. This can be an effective way to overcome feelings of helplessness and paralysis that often come with self-criticism. Once we recognize the inner critic behind our turmoil, we can take action to neutralize its attacks.

In Anna's case, *talking back* can be an effective way to counteract her inner critic,

- *Are you trying to convince me that I can't write this essay and that I shouldn't even try just to avoid the risk of failing?*
- *Are you protecting me from the fear of failure by persuading me to give up? If so, how will I ever learn new things and grow?*
- *If I get an average mark for this essay, does it mean I'm worthless?*
- *So are you trying to protect my reputation and spare me from humiliation by others? Is that compassion, or just plain denigration?*

Talking back can be an effective way to expose the distorted assumptions behind the critic's attacks, thereby silencing it:

- *Are you telling me that if I'm not perfect all the time, I'm a failure?*
- *Because I made a mistake, does it make me a worthless person?*
- *Would achieving my goal add value to my person?*
- *If people are not pleased with me, does it mean I'm worthless?*
- *You're comparing me to him to make me work harder, aren't you?*
- *I already did my best in the circumstances; do I need a kicker like you?*

We can tell Jesus about the inner critic because the Lord is the compassionate presence who is closer to us than even the critic's judging voice.

8
Resistance and Surrender

On August 15, 1975, Archbishop Francis Xavier Nguyen Van Thuan was invited to the Presidential Palace at 2 p.m. and arrested by the Vietnamese Communist Government. Soon after his arrest, he made a crucial decision. He wrote, "That night, as the police drove me along the 450-kilometer road that brought me to my place of detention, many emotions came to me: sadness, loneliness, exhaustion after three stressful months....But one thought broke through clearly to disperse all the darkness, the words of Monsignor John Walsh, an American missionary bishop in China who said when he was released after 12 years of imprisonment: 'I have spent half my life waiting.' It's so true! All prisoners, myself included, spend every moment waiting for freedom. After thinking it over in that white Toyota, I made a decision: I would not wait. I would live in the present moment and fill it with love."[1]

This decision affected his attitude and way of life during his long years in confinement and for the remainder of his life. He wrote:

> Lord, I will not wait,
> I choose to live in the present moment,
> And fill it with love.
> Just like one dot following another,
> Thousands of dots form a long line,

THE BREATH OF CHRIST

One minute following another,
Millions of minutes become one life.
Dot each dot correctly, the line will be beautiful.
Live each minute well; one's life will be holy.

SURRENDER AS THE KEY TO PEACE

In the midst of adversity and inner turmoil, Archbishop Francis found peace through surrender. Similarly, millions of people worldwide struggling with alcohol addiction have found peace and a new start in life with the Alcoholics Anonymous (AA) programs through surrender. People with terminal illnesses who are apprehensive about their imminent death can find peace through surrender.

Since the concept of surrender can often cause confusion, it is important to examine what surrender is and how it works in different contexts.

When we are faced with a difficult situation, surrender means letting go of the illusion that we have complete control over it. This illusion of control is often the cause of stress and anxiety in our lives. Resistance means holding on to this illusion and fighting frantically to stay in control. By surrendering, we accept that we do not have total control over everything in our lives, nor do we have to. This acceptance leads to a sense of lightness, peace, rest, and joy as we stop fighting against reality and open ourselves up to new possibilities.

In Christian spirituality, surrendering means submitting to God, who is referred to as the power greater than ourselves in the AA program. It is to accept that we are not all-powerful and cannot do everything on our own. Surrendering involves letting go of our resistance and allowing God to take control of our lives. It is about acknowledging our limitations as human beings and recognizing the ultimate power of God.

Resistance and Surrender

In the face of adversity or injustice, surrendering does not mean giving up and doing nothing. We do not surrender to the adverse event but to God, who is in control even in the midst of adversity. Through surrender, we can accept the choices available in a given situation, no matter how limited they may be, and focus our energy on the work at hand. When you surrender, you accept that the event that occurred is beyond your control. What is within your control is how you respond to it. Surrendering means accepting the choices available to you in the face of such an adverse event.

SURRENDER AND ALCOHOL ADDICTION

Perhaps the most pertinent testimonies of the power of surrender come from those struggling with addiction. For members of the AA program, surrender means acknowledging that they have a problem that is beyond their control. It involves accepting the fact that they are powerless over their alcohol consumption, and as a result, many aspects of their lives are unmanageable. They choose to submit to a power greater than themselves. A woman in the program shared her experience,

> The fellowship I found in A.A. enabled me to face my problem honestly and squarely....No one likes to admit that they're a drunk, that they can't control this thing....I went to closed meetings and open meetings....It was at that point that I reached surrender. I heard one very ill woman say that she didn't believe in the surrender part of the A.A. program. My heavens! Surrender to me has meant the ability to run my home, to face my responsibilities as they should be faced, to take life as it comes to me day by day and work my problems out. That's what surrender has meant to me.[2]

THE BREATH OF CHRIST

For individuals struggling with alcohol addiction, the belief that they are in control of their drinking often creates a false sense of security. They might tell themselves that they can stop drinking anytime they want, that alcohol helps them manage stress, or that they only need it as a temporary aid until they get their life sorted out. Unfortunately, this illusion keeps them in denial about the severity of their problem, leading them to rationalize their behavior and make excuses rather than admit they need help. This denial can prevent them from recognizing that they are unable to control their drinking or manage many aspects of their life, such as finances, job performance, health, relationships, and family. To break free from this cycle, they must let go of their illusion of control, admit that they have a problem, seek help from a higher power, and take responsibility for their actions.

For many who struggle with alcohol, shame can be a factor affecting their drinking. They feel ashamed that they are not able to control their drinking, when they cannot be a supportive spouse or parent, or when they do not earn money to support their family. This self-criticism and shame can be overwhelming and painful, leading to a need to drink to soothe the pain. However, this temporary relief only brings even more shame afterward, trapping them in a vicious cycle that perpetuates drinking.

In this situation, being in control is felt as a demand, causing them to be ashamed of themselves for falling short of that demand. Surrendering means acknowledging that they are not in complete control but also recognizing that they need not do it alone. Instead, they can turn to a higher power for assistance and guidance rather than demanding that they control their life alone and feeling ashamed because of their repeated failure.

Once people admit to their problems and surrender to a higher power, they can take responsibility for their actions and focus their energy on making the most of the choices available to them. That critical step gives them a fresh start in life.

Resistance and Surrender

SURRENDER AND IMMINENT DEATH

Dr. Elisabeth Kübler-Ross shared a poignant story of a young boy who found peace when he was dying from a terminal illness. Initially, he expressed his inner turmoil when he drew a picture of himself as a tiny figure about to be hit by a large cannonball. The doctor reported his subsequent progress:

> After we worked together for a while, he accepted and surrendered to what was happening in his body. I knew our work was done when he drew a picture of himself flying on the wings of a bird to heaven. Now he felt a loving force would carry him off; he wouldn't resist it. This surrender made the rest of his life, however brief, more enjoyable and meaningful.[3]

In her influential 1969 book *On Death and Dying*, Kübler-Ross outlined the five stages that individuals experience when facing imminent death: denial, anger, bargaining, depression, and acceptance.[4] Through her extensive work with dying patients, Kübler-Ross observed that people often find it difficult to come to terms with death, which leads to immense suffering as they move through the initial stages of dying. However, with the support of loved ones, palliative care, and pastoral guidance, the dying person can navigate through these stages of resistance and ultimately arrive at a peaceful acceptance of death.

Kübler-Ross described the stage of acceptance as a time when the patient is often tired and weak and requires frequent and short intervals of sleep. It is as if the pain has gone, and the struggle is over. The patient has attained peace in acceptance. They are no longer stirred up by news or problems of the outer world. They prefer to be left alone, and their transition will be smoother if they are allowed to detach themselves gradually from all meaningful relationships in their life. At this stage, their family usually needs more help, guidance, and support to accept the patient's impending death in the same way.[5]

SURRENDER AND DOMESTIC VIOLENCE

Although domestic violence can be perpetrated by both men and women, in the majority of cases, women suffer violence at the hands of their intimate partners. Many women remain in abusive relationships due to fear. Some fear being harmed by their abuser if they leave, while others fear losing their children or being unable to support themselves and their children. When abuse happens, the victim might blame herself or make excuses for her abuser's behavior. She might recall the honeymoon phase when her partner was charming, caring, and supportive. She might think that maybe his anger is simply due to stress. She might try harder to avoid triggering his rage, reasoning that if she acts differently, *she* can stop the abuse. In other words, she believes that his abusive behavior is *her* fault, which is in line with the abuser's habit of blaming the victim. Moreover, she might feel ashamed to admit that the man she loves is terrorizing her or might not even realize that she is a victim of abuse.[6]

Fear, denial, self-blame, and shame all contribute to women staying in abusive relationships. Perhaps the most devastating is the idea that she can change her abuser's behavior by changing herself. This is the illusion of control, turned against oneself. She tells herself that she can control the situation. By becoming the person he wants her to be, the perfect wife, she can stop the abuse. In doing this, she takes responsibility for his behavior and harms herself even more.

In the context of domestic abuse, surrender does not mean condoning the abuse or submitting to the abuser's control. Instead, it means accepting that his abusive behavior is beyond her control.

Resistance and Surrender

She cannot change his behavior by changing herself, nor can she stop his violence by making herself smaller or more subservient. Surrendering means submitting herself to God and asking for guidance and support to keep herself and her children safe. This often involves seeking help from the right people and agencies and forming a safety plan as the first step. Since domestic violence thrives on secrecy, disclosing it to others is a healthy step forward. When there is adequate support to ensure her safety, the abuser needs to be held accountable for his behavior. The next steps will depend on whether he is willing to take responsibility for his actions and make real changes to ensure safety in the home. In some cases, leaving the relationship might be the only way to ensure the safety of the woman and her children.[7]

SURRENDER AND POSITIVE ACTION

As spiritual author Eckhart Tolle points out, surrender is compatible with making plans and taking positive action in the face of adversity or injustice.[8] It does not mean accepting defeat and doing nothing. Surrender refers to the inner attitude with which you approach your life situation and how you act to create positive change.

As Tolle explains, when facing an adverse situation, you have three options: remove yourself from it, change it, or accept it totally. If you cannot change or leave the situation, the best approach is to let go of any resistance and accept it as if you had chosen it. This is the most sensible way to deal with the situation.[9]

When Archbishop Francis was arrested, he chose to surrender to God and live in the present moment. This did not mean that he approved of his arrest, as surrender does not imply approval. As he could neither change the situation nor remove himself from it, he accepted that he had no control over it. He let go of all inner resistance and adapted to his life situation. By doing so, he could focus his energy on making the most of the choices available to him while in detention instead of dwelling in frustration and waiting for his release to resume living.[10]

Once you have surrendered, your actions will be infused with a new quality of awareness and peacefulness. Tolle calls this positive action or surrendered action, which is far more effective than negative action that arises from anger, frustration, or despair. You will experience lightness and tranquility in what you do. If none of these options are available, surrendering means accepting the situation without resentment, judgment, or blame. In any case, surrender is the key to inner peace.

RESISTANCE AND SUFFERING

Resistance is the act of mentally judging and rejecting the fact that you are in the current situation. It is the root cause of all negativity, such as irritation, impatience, anger, rage, resentment, and despair.[11] Put another way, resistance is at the core of *suffering*. Medically speaking, pain and suffering are two distinct concepts. The International Association for the Study of Pain (IASP) defines *physical* pain as "an unpleasant sensory and emotional experience associated with, or resembling that associated with, actual or potential tissue damage."[12] Psychological pain refers to the experience of perceived injury to or diminishment of the self. In distinction, *suffering* refers to the subjective experience of pain *and* inner resistance to it. In other words, suffering is the experience of pain plus the resistance to pain.[13] To put it simply:

Suffering = Pain + Resistance

Surrender is most significant when we face a major life catastrophe. This may include a major illness or disability, loss of employment or possessions, bereavement, or imminent death. In such

Resistance and Surrender

situations, we have no control over what happens to us, and we cannot remove ourselves from it. Two choices are available to us: we can either fight against the fact that it is happening or accept and adapt ourselves to it. Resistance causes further suffering, while surrender is the key to peace.

Pain + Surrender = Peace

When we stop resisting the present moment, negative thoughts and emotions will not arise. This means that difficult external circumstances will not cause us more unhappiness. Instead, by relinquishing inner resistance, we can live peacefully and freely, even in the face of adversity. In this state of surrender, a different kind of energy flows into our activity, making it more effective. Tolle maintains that surrender is the most important thing we can do to bring about positive changes in the world. Surrender is primary, and any action we take is secondary.

Surrender is also an effective way to weaken our ego or false self. The ego thrives on resistance because it fuels its need to be distinct from and superior to others. Strangely, the ego loves to harbor negativity because it believes that negativity will get it what it wants.[14] The ego tends to perceive resistance as a sign of strength. The fact is that resistance disconnects us from God, the only source of true power. Each time we surrender, the ego, the false, unhappy self that loves feeling miserable, resentful, or sorry for itself, will be deprived of its lifeblood.[15] The practice of surrender liberates us from the need to depend on ego defenses and false facades. We become simpler and more authentic.

GOD'S BOUNDLESS TREASURES

From a Christian spiritual perspective, the practice of surrender can also open the door to God's boundless treasures. This is because we live in a world of God's abundant graces, which constantly nourish and transform us. The only point at which we can access God's graces and nourishment is the Now. In the spiritual classic *Abandonment to Divine Providence*, Jean-Pierre de Caussade refers to God's boundless graces working invisibly underneath all that is presented to us in the present moment. We can access God's invisible graces by fulfilling our duties and lovingly accepting everything that God sends our way, including the attractions and challenges we face in each moment. For this reason, even the simplest activities, such as washing the dishes, cleaning the house, or reading to one's child, can unleash God's infinite graces. The present moment is regarded as a sacrament because it mediates God's grace through the ordinary duties and events of everyday life. It is where human activity meets God's activity and becomes enlivened by it.

De Caussade stresses that the events of every moment reflect the will of God and his holy name. Therefore, they should be treated with the greatest reverence. Everything that bears God's holy name is manna from heaven that nurtures our souls and sanctifies us if we do not obstruct it.[16] For those who know where to look,

> the treasure is everywhere, it is offered to us at all times and wherever we may be. All creatures, both friends and enemies, pour it out with prodigality, and it flows like a fountain through every faculty of body and soul even to the very center of our hearts. If we open our mouths they will be filled. The divine activity permeates the whole universe, it pervades every creature; wherever they are it is there; it goes before them, with them, and it follows them; all they have to do is to let the waves bear them on.[17]

De Caussade sums up the requirements of sanctity in a single practice: fidelity to the duties appointed by God in each moment.

Resistance and Surrender

This is the central tenet of his spirituality. The practice of fidelity has two aspects: active and passive.

First, the active practice of fidelity involves performing the duties that are assigned to us, whether they are mandated by the laws of God, the Church, or the particular state of life we have chosen. Second, the passive practice of fidelity, also known as surrender or abandonment, involves accepting everything that comes our way with reverence and equanimity. This includes accepting events beyond our control despite the weariness and disgust they may cause.

De Caussade's teachings on abandonment are in line with Tolle's view on surrender. Surrender is the crucial path to achieving inner peace and living in the present moment, a powerful tool to overcome the ego, and a way to put an end to suffering. It is also the key to experiencing joy and spiritual transformation.

SURRENDER AND THE JESUS PRAYER

Though we can easily grasp the importance of surrender, it is not always easy to put it into practice. In the face of major life challenges, our natural response is often resistance, not surrender. The Jesus Prayer can be a powerful path to transforming our reactivity and negative emotions into prayer, opening the path to surrender.

- *Lord, I just lost my job. This is so stressful because I am the primary provider for my family. I am very upset and disappointed with myself. I am anxious about how to support my family. Lord Jesus, help me!*
- *Lord, since my back injury, I haven't been able to work and have to depend on my children. I am so depressed because I don't want to be a burden to my children. Lord Jesus, help me!*

THE BREATH OF CHRIST

* *Lord, my young son is very sick with a chest infection. He is very distressed in the hospital. I am worried about him and feel so helpless. Lord Jesus, help me!*

Through this prayer, we can transition from a state of fear and vulnerability to one of love and safety in God's presence. Instead of resisting in fear, we can learn to surrender with love and unlock the treasure God has in store for us in difficult times. This allows us to focus our attention and energy on making positive changes in the world.

9

Letting Go of Our Ego

After a retreat on the Jesus Prayer, Chelsea wrote, "From the very first evening, I felt safe and surrounded by Abba's abundant love in this sacred space. My desire was to meet God and have him as my companion. I had learned the Jesus Prayer before, but I had never experienced its power. However, when I saw the skit 'Agents of Darkness,' I realized that the enemy had interfered in my spiritual life, causing me to lose heart and give up on prayer, even doubting God's existence. It was as if the skit was speaking directly to me! Lord Jesus, help me! Thus began my journey home. Along the way, I realized the many burdens I had been carrying and how I had been consumed by worries about imminent dangers that never actually happened. I also recognized the various faces of my ego: the prideful ego looking down on people; the self-pity ego blaming others for its unhappiness; the self-loathing ego immersed in an inferiority complex and self-blame. I saw myself easily getting caught up in them at different times. It's wonderful to notice the many faces of your ego, laugh at it, and realize its destructive games. What good does it ever bring? Lord Jesus, help me! It's time to come down from self-inflation, rise up from self-pity and self-criticism, stand with my feet on the ground, and be myself with my brothers and sisters. Lord Jesus, help me!"

EGO: THE MIND-GENERATED SELF

In Christian spirituality, the term "ego" refers to the false self or the fallen self. It is synonymous with egocentricity or self-centeredness.

THE BREATH OF CHRIST

It is considered the biggest obstacle in our spiritual journey and the number-one enemy of relationships and community. In his introduction to Augustine's *City of God*, Thomas Merton refers to original sin as an act of spiritual apostasy by which humans fall from the blessed state of union with God into falsehood, division, and disharmony. From this fall, each self-centered individual becomes their own little god.[1] Humans become divided against one another and fight endless battles to assert their importance, impose their will on others, and compete for resources on this earth.

But where does the ego come from? To gain a better understanding of the ego, it is helpful to know its origins and the purpose it serves in our lives. It all begins with the mind, the control center managing both information and energy, which is responsible for our survival by safeguarding and nurturing us. To ensure our survival, the mind generates a mental image of ourselves as distinct individuals, separate from others. This mind-generated image is known as the ego. Once it is formed, we tend to become strongly attached to our ego, often identifying ourselves with it and believing it to be who we are. Unfortunately, this is where the mind's biggest mistake lies. It assumes that the ego is our true self, which leads to endless errors in perception and judgment about ourselves and the world around us.

In essence, the ego is a construct of the mind, fueled by our psychic energy and strengthened by the attention and praise from others. As we get attached to it, we become anxious because we realize how fragile it is. The ego then becomes the driving force behind our fight for survival. It urges us to affirm ourselves and consolidate our identity. When we mistakenly identify ourselves with the ego, it becomes the center of our lives. Our thoughts and actions start to revolve around it. We become self-centered and obsessed with our interests, rights, and happiness.

We often identify ourselves with our ego without even realizing it. As a result, we start to desire what it desires and fear what it fears. As the ego is driven by fear, we become fearful for as long as we are in its control. We are consumed by its fear of being ordinary, small, or insignificant. We are driven by its need to stand out, be better, and have more than others. Whenever the ego feels threatened, it reacts violently, much like a wounded animal fighting for survival. The ego is always afraid of being destroyed, and as a result, it tries to assert its importance and superiority in every possible way. Despite boasting of its own goodness and importance, the ego also worries about its fragility and imperfection. When controlled by the ego, we live in the illusion that we are separate from everything. We are cut off from the joy of being connected to the source of life and love that lives in all things. This sense of separation leads to unhappiness, loneliness, and fear.[2]

The ego is the primary cause of fear, self-interest, and the desire for power. It can take many forms, but it is always driven by the same motivation: to distinguish itself, to stand out, to have control, and to accumulate more. The ego is seldom content with what it has, leading to endless frustration and dissatisfaction. Negative emotions such as anger, anxiety, hatred, resentment, dissatisfaction, and jealousy often stem from the ego.[3] When we are self-centered, we disconnect ourselves from everything and everyone around us. However, when we practice compassion toward ourselves and others, we open ourselves to the divine source of compassion and can channel God's compassion into the world.

THREE CATEGORIES OF EGOISTIC BEHAVIORS

It is helpful to explore three common categories of egoistic behaviors: self-inflation, self-pity, and self-loathing.

Perhaps the most common behavior of the ego is self-inflation. When the ego is inflated, it sees itself as superior to others. This leads to arrogance, boastfulness, and looking down on others. It is a selfish and entitled posture that believes it deserves admiration, praise, and care due to its sheer talents and goodness. Ego-driven individuals believe other people exist solely to serve them and make them happy. They often take credit for things that go well, even if they are not solely responsible for them. They tend to blame others for their own failures or misdeeds. These individuals are highly competitive and become jealous when others receive more recognition or affection. For them, life is a zero-sum game. They believe there is never enough to go around: the other's gain is their loss.

In addition, ego-inflated individuals would never say "Thank you" or "Sorry" to anyone. They do not express gratitude because they take people for granted and believe that others are only doing what is expected of them. Moreover, they think they are not receiving the services they are entitled to. For instance, an egoistic husband would view his wife and children as people who exist to serve him. He, therefore, believes that he deserves all the attention and care he receives from them and more. He never appreciates them for what they do for him but always demands more from them. Egoistic people will never apologize because they are never wrong. Even when they make mistakes, they will either deny it, shift blame to other people, or try to explain it away instead of admitting to their wrongdoing.

Another common behavior of the ego is self-pity. In this posture, the ego is filled with grief for its misery and lack, and it blames other people for its unhappiness. Similar to self-inflation, the self-pitying ego views itself as superior to others and believes it deserves admiration, attention, and care from others. However, it is consumed in sorrow and resentment because it does not receive the treatment it thinks it deserves. The ego often engages in an internal dialogue that goes like this, "Nobody cares about me. Everyone seems so selfish and preoccupied with their own lives that they don't even notice how miserable I am. I am so unhappy, and it's all their fault. They only care about themselves and their

Letting Go of Our Ego

interests. But what about me? Am I nothing to them? Don't I deserve their attention and care? After all the things I've done for them, this is how they repay me?" Self-pity is the endless pit that sucks in its victims and generates nothing but misery, frustration, and blame.

Self-loathing is also a manifestation of the ego. The self-loathing ego views itself as inferior to others and despises itself for it. This is known as having low self-esteem in psychology. In chapter 8, we discussed how individuals with low self-esteem tend to be ashamed of themselves because they believe they have no value and are unworthy of respect, friendship, and belonging. They tend to avoid facing problems instead of expressing their opinions or needs, and are hesitant to ask for help. They avoid situations where they risk failure, criticism, or rejection. They are highly sensitive to feedback, and small criticisms from others can lead to an emotional breakdown because of their habit of self-judgment.

In addition, individuals who suffer from self-loathing often experience an inner conflict between self-preservation and self-punishment. Remember that the mind's responsibility is to ensure the individual's survival, and this is the drive for self-preservation. However, in the case of a self-loathing individual, the mind dislikes and even hates the ego, and this creates a drive for self-punishment or self-neglect. This drive for self-punishment diametrically opposes the drive for self-preservation. Self-loathing individuals are caught in a civil war between these opposing forces. They often struggle between self-care and self-neglect, self-enjoyment and self-punishment, and the pursuit of happiness and self-sabotage. As we discussed in chapter 8, self-loathing can lead to depression, anxiety disorders, and self-harm.

Each of these egoistic postures is a significant barrier to intimacy in relationships. The self-inflated ego pushes other people away because it looks down upon them and often seeks to control, manipulate, or exploit them for its own benefit. The ego that is filled with self-pity distances itself from others by drowning itself in sorrow, resentment, and blame. Lastly, the ego that is consumed by self-hatred views itself as undeserving of belonging and intimate relationships and thus tends to isolate itself from any meaningful connection with others.

Spiritual writers refer to the ego as the illusory self because, in reality, we do not exist separately from all things. We do not need to constantly strive for survival or validate our existence by being better than others. Once we realize that the ego is an illusion, we can let go of these erroneous notions and return to our true selves. This shift allows lightness, peace, and joy to enter our lives.

Since the ego is an illusion, it dissolves when exposed to the light of consciousness. Our ego can easily control us because we are not aware of it. Once we become aware of our ego and its harmful habits, it loses its power over us. When we are truly present in what we are doing, we are aware of our thoughts and actions, and we consciously choose to act instead of acting out of habit or under the control of the ego.

For individuals with an inflated ego, it might come as a relief to know that all their efforts to stand out, to exalt themselves, and to accumulate more are simply unnecessary for survival or true happiness. Inflating the illusory self does not bring happiness, only momentary satisfaction, along with enormous harm to themselves and others. From this realization, what remains for them is the process of recognizing and letting go of the egoistic habits of thought and judgment regarding themselves and others.

For individuals with self-pity, they must recognize and let go of the harmful habit of blaming others for their misery that invariably leads them down the pit of resentment and more misery. Overcoming this habit might begin with the person's realization that it is an exhausting habit that never does them any good, only harm. Having realized this, they must build a fence around that pit of self-pity and guard themselves against the thought habits that can push them toward it.

For individuals struggling with self-hatred, it can be comforting to know that the negative image they hold of themselves is not their true self but rather a creation of their own mind. Put simply, their mind has generated a mental image of themselves that they dislike. Their self-hatred is not a reflection of their true worth but rather a result of their habitual tendency to judge and reject themselves. Once they grasp this concept, they can begin to let go of these pathological mental habits and instead cultivate healthy habits of self-compassion. When they truly let go of their self-hatred, they will stop judging, rejecting, neglecting, or punishing themselves. This will put an end to the internal conflict they experience. They can learn to treat themselves with kindness, empathy, and compassion.

BREAKING FREE FROM EGOISTIC BONDAGE

Recognizing and understanding the various faces and strategies of the ego is a significant milestone toward freedom from its bondage, as it implies separating the ego—our false self—from who we are. It is an awakening to the fact that our ego is just an illusion, and its drives do not necessarily align with our interests. The remaining challenge is to learn how the ego manifests itself in our daily thought and judgment patterns and to free ourselves from its grasp.

Overcoming a well-established habit is challenging, and the same goes for egoistic habits. We must constantly review our thoughts, judgments, emotions, and behaviors to overcome such habits. As we do this regularly, we develop an "ego detector" that becomes more sensitive to the various manifestations of the ego. In Ignatian spirituality, this is referred to as the awareness examen. It involves prayerfully reflecting on our own thoughts and behaviors to identify whether our ego was behind the need to stand out, be right in an argument, or our desire to counteract a perceived attack.

The Jesus Prayer is useful for sorting out complex and conflicting emotions. It can also help us overcome the egoistic need to judge, blame, or counterattack.

- *Lord, I was so upset when that person corrected me in front of others. I wanted to show them how smart and educated I was. Lord Jesus, help me!*
- *Lord, I realize I have taken my wife for granted and hardly ever thanked her for what she has done for me. Lord Jesus, help me!*
- *Lord, I feel very uncomfortable when my coworker gets a bigger bonus than me. Lord Jesus, help me!*
- *Lord, I couldn't bear it when my neighbor boasted about her son receiving a college scholarship. I was jealous of her. Lord Jesus, help me!*
- *Lord, when I am unhappy, I often blame my parents for not caring enough for me. Lord Jesus, help me!*
- *Lord, I can't stop blaming myself when someone criticizes me. I hold myself to high standards all the time and can't tolerate any mistakes or failures. Lord Jesus, help me!*

By naming your egoistic reactions and behaviors and seeking assistance from the Lord, you gradually bring your ego more fully to the light of Christ's presence and free yourself from its grip. When falsehood is exposed to this divine light, it dissolves. As you and Christ take back more and more of your inner self from the ego's control, you feel greater freedom and peace, while fear is replaced by love and endless joy.

Coming Home

Elizabeth Kübler-Ross made a profound observation about the human condition when she wrote that there is only love or fear.[1] She described love and fear as two mutually exclusive places. The place of love is where we find happiness, contentment, peace, and joy. On the other hand, the place of fear is where we find anger, hate, anxiety, and guilt.

The place of love is our true home, where we experience happiness, joy, and peace. In this space, we are connected with God, the infinite source of love and light. It is the place of abundance where God cares for us intimately and provides for our needs.

On the other hand, the place of fear is where we are estranged from home. It is a realm with a pervasive sense of danger and loneliness, where you are consumed by negative emotions like anxiety, anger, shame, self-criticism, and hurt. It is a world of scarcity and privation, where we feel we have to compete against others for survival. It is the realm of the ego.

Unfortunately, we often find ourselves in the place of fear. We struggle with worries about ourselves, work, relationships, and family. We find ourselves in the shadows of our past hurts. We are prone to stress and easily triggered to anger and rage. We are afflicted with endless self-criticism and react against adverse life situations. This seems to be where we have all spent most of our lives.

The good news is that we have a choice about where we want to be. The Jesus Prayer is a pathway that enables us to come home each time we catch ourselves in the space of fear. By invoking the Lord's name in faith and trust, we have unlimited access to God's

THE BREATH OF CHRIST

gift of salvation in Christ. Wherever we find ourselves, the prayer can help us come home to the place of love, happiness, peace, and joy.

This book offers insights into the spaces of fear where you may feel disconnected from God's love and light. I hope these insights will help you understand these places of estrangement better so that you can recognize them more easily in your own life and find your way home.

Notes

INTRODUCTION

1. *The Way of a Pilgrim: and the Pilgrim Continues his Way*, trans. R. M. French (London: SPCK, 2012), 15.
2. French, *The Way of a Pilgrim*, 27.
3. French, *The Way of a Pilgrim*, 118.

CHAPTER 1

1. Kallistos Ware, *The Jesus Prayer* (London: Catholic Truth Society, 2014), 5–6.
2. Ware, *The Jesus Prayer*, 6–8.
3. G. E. H. Palmer, Philip Sherrard, and Kallistos Ware, trans. and eds., *The Philokalia: The Complete Text Compiled by St. Nikodimos of the Holy Mountain and St. Makarios of Corinth*, vol. 1 (Boston: Faber and Faber, 2011), 270, Kindle.
4. Palmer et al., *The Philokalia*, 1:270–6.
5. Brock Bingaman and Bradley Nassif, eds., *The Philokalia: A Classic Text of Orthodox Spirituality* (New York: Oxford University Press, 2012), 194–95.
6. Bingaman, *The Philokalia*, 2:347. John F. Gill, *To Call on His Name: Perspectives on the Jesus Prayer* (Durham, NC: Sacristy Press, 2019), 37.
7. Palmer et al., *The Philokalia*, 1:63.
8. Ware, *The Jesus Prayer*, 10.
9. Ware, *The Jesus Prayer*, 13.

10. Gill, *To Call on His Name*, 110–11.
11. Gill, *To Call on His Name*, 112–23.
12. G. E. H. Palmer, Philip Sherrard, and Kallistos Ware, trans. and ed., *The Philokalia: The Complete Text Compiled by St. Nikodimos of the Holy Mountain and St. Makarios of Corinth*, vol. 4 (Boston: Faber and Faber, 2010), 238. Kallistos Ware, "The Jesus Prayer in St Gregory of Sinai," *Eastern Churches Review* 4, no. 1 (1972): 3–22, 4.
13. Palmer et al., *The Philokalia*, 4:259.
14. Ware, "The Jesus Prayer in St Gregory of Sinai," 7–8.
15. See Palmer et al., *The Philokalia*, 1: Glossary.
16. Ware, *The Jesus Prayer*, 36
17. Ware, "The Jesus Prayer in St Gregory of Sinai," 9.
18. Ware, *The Jesus Prayer*, 15
19. Ware, *The Jesus Prayer*, 29
20. Ware, *The Jesus Prayer*, 29.
21. Ware, *The Jesus Prayer*, 30.
22. Ware, *The Jesus Prayer*, 32.
23. Ware, *The Jesus Prayer*, 32.
24. Palmer et al., *The Philokalia*, 4:210.
25. Ware, "The Jesus Prayer in St Gregory of Sinai," 4.
26. Ware, *The Jesus Prayer*, 24.
27. Ware, *The Jesus Prayer*, 24.
28. Ware, *The Jesus Prayer*, 25.

CHAPTER 2

1. Fung Yu-Lan, *A Short History of Chinese Philosophy* (New York: The Free Press, 1966), 69–70.
2. Fung, *A Short History of Chinese Philosophy*, 157–62.
3. G. E. H. Palmer, Philip Sherrard, and Kallistos Ware, trans. and ed., *The Philokalia: The Complete Text Compiled by St. Nikodi-*

mos of the Holy Mountain and St. Makarios of Corinth, vol. 4 (Boston: Faber and Faber, 2010), 4:259.

    4. Palmer et al., *The Philokalia*, 4:259.
    5. Palmer et al., *The Philokalia*, 4:259.
    6. Palmer et al., *The Philokalia*, 4:260.
    7. Palmer et al., *The Philokalia*, 4:260.
    8. Palmer et al., *The Philokalia*, 4:262.
    9. Palmer et al., *The Philokalia*, 4:262.
    10. Palmer et al., *The Philokalia*, 4:262.
    11. Palmer et al., *The Philokalia*, 4:270.
    12. Palmer et al., *The Philokalia*, 4:270–71.

CHAPTER 3

1. Tony Schwartz, with Jean Gomes and Catherine McCarthy, *The Way We're Working Isn't Working* (New York: Simon & Schuster, 2010), chap. 10, Kindle.

2. Daniel J. Siegel, *Mindsight: Change Your Brain and Your Life* (Melbourne: Scribe Publications, 2012), 115.

    3. Siegel, *Mindsight*, 116.
    4. Siegel, *Mindsight*, 116.
    5. Siegel, *Mindsight*, 53.

CHAPTER 4

1. Dale Carnegie, *Quẳng Gánh Lo Đi và Vui Sống*, trans. Nguyễn Hiến Lê and P. Hiếu (Saigon: Khai Trí, 1951). This translation has been reprinted and reproduced in many forms.

2. American Psychiatric Association, *Diagnostic and Statistical Manual of Mental Disorders*, 5th ed. (Washington DC: American Psychiatric Publishing, 2013), 189.

3. Cf. Judson Brewer, *Unwinding Anxiety: New Science Shows How to Break the Cycles of Worry and Fear to Heal Your Mind* (New York: Penguin Random House, 2021), 88–89.

4. David Semple and Roger Smyth, *Oxford Handbook of Psychiatry* (New York: Oxford University Press, 2019), 166.

5. There is a debate in psychology on whether there is such a thing as good anxiety. I think a significant part of this debate is about terminology. If we accept the idea of a threshold of anxious arousal, the question becomes, "What do we call the level of arousal below this threshold?" Those who deny the idea of "good anxiety," like Judson Brewer, would not call arousal below this threshold "anxiety." In other words, only when arousal reaches a certain level can it be called anxiety, and it is always bad because it impairs mental and physical performance. See Brewer, *Unwinding Anxiety*, 151–59.

6. The School of Life, *Anxiety: Meditations on the Anxious Mind* (London: The School of Life, 2020).

7. Brewer, *Unwinding Anxiety*.

8. Brewer points out that this is the function of the prefrontal cortex, the part of the brain closest to our forehead. Brewer, *Unwinding Anxiety*, 31.

9. Dale Carnegie, *How to Stop Worrying and Start Living* (New Delhi: Diamond Pocket Books, 2016), Kindle.

10. Carnegie, *How to Stop Worrying*, chap. 5.

11. Carnegie, *How to Stop Worrying*, chap. 13.

12. For an insightful treatment of these issues, see the School of Life, *Anxiety*.

13. Charles Duhigg, *The Power of Habit: Why We Do What We Do in Life and Business* (New York: Random House, 2012), 52–53.

14. Brewer, *Unwinding Anxiety*, 79–80.

15. Brewer uses the more neutral terms for the three elements of the habit loop: Trigger, Behavior, and Result. Brewer, *Unwinding Anxiety*, 46.

16. Brewer, *Unwinding Anxiety*, 42–51.

Notes

CHAPTER 5

1. Gilbert Reyes, Jon D. Elhai, and Julian D. Ford, eds., *The Encyclopedia of Psychological Trauma* (Hoboken, NJ: John Wiley & Sons, 2008), x.

2. "IASP Announces Revised Definition of Pain," published July 16, 2020, https://www.iasp-pain.org/PublicationsNews/NewsDetail.aspx?ItemNumber=10475.

3. For a more thorough treatment of the clinical features of psychological trauma and its impact, see American Psychiatric Association, *Diagnostic and Statistical Manual of Mental Disorders*, 5th ed. (Washington DC: American Psychiatric Publishing, 2013), 271–86.

4. "The prevalence of acute stress disorder in recently trauma-exposed populations (i.e., within 1 month of trauma exposure) varies according to the nature of the event and the context in which it is assessed. In both U.S. and non-U.S. populations, acute stress disorder tends to be identified in less than 20% of cases following traumatic events that do not involve interpersonal assault; 13%–21% of motor vehicle accidents, 14% of mild traumatic brain injury, 19% of assault, 10% of severe burns, and 6%–12% of industrial accidents. Higher rates (i.e., 20%–50%) are reported following interpersonal traumatic events, including assault, rape, and witnessing a mass shooting." American Psychiatric Association, *Diagnostic and Statistical Manual of Mental Disorders*, 284.

5. American Psychiatric Association, *Diagnostic and Statistical Manual of Mental Disorders*, 277.

6. Reyes et al., *Encyclopedia of Psychological Trauma*, xi.

7. Thich Nhat Hanh, *Peace Is Every Step: The Path of Mindfulness in Everyday Life*, ed. Arnold Kotler (New York: Bantam Books, 1991), 64–65.

8. Thich Nhat Hanh, *Peace Is Every Step*, 65–66.

9. Thich Nhat Hanh, Satsang in Vietnamese, "Ru Nội Kết—Thực Tập Trong Bản Môn," March 16, 1995, at Plum Village,

posted November 28, 2017, https://www.youtube.com/watch?v=V28QGpMuun4.

10. Eckhart Tolle, *The Power of Now: A Guide to Spiritual Enlightenment* (Vancouver, BC: Namaste Publishing and Novato, CA: New World Library, 1999/2004), 36–39. Kindle.

11. Thich Nhat Hanh makes a similar point in *Peace Is Every Step*, 62–63. He uses the image of cooking potatoes: the process through which raw potatoes (negative feelings) are heated on a fire (mindfulness) to become edible food (good energy).

12. Thomas Keating, *Open Minds, Open Hearts: The Contemplative Dimension of the Gospel* (New York: Continuum, 1995), 120.

13. Thomas Keating, *On Divine Therapy* (New York: Lantern Books, 2012), Kindle.

14. D. W. Winnicott, *Psycho-Analytic Explorations*, ed. Clare Winnicott, Ray Shepherd, Madeleine Davis (New York: Routledge, 2018), 87–95.

CHAPTER 6

1. Harriet Lerner, *The Dance of Anger: A Woman's Guide to Changing the Patterns of Intimate Relationships* (New York: HarperCollins, 1985/2014), 1, Kindle.

2. Aaron Karmin, *Anger Management Workbook for Men: Take Control of Your Anger and Master Your Emotions* (Berkeley, CA: Althea Press, 2016), 66–67.

3. Cf. Karmin, *Anger Management Workbook for Men*, 71.

4. Matthew McKay, Peter D. Rogers, and Judith McKay, *When Anger Hurts: Quieting the Storm Within*, 2nd ed. (Oakland, CA: New Harbinger Publications, 2003), 80–95.

5. McKay et al., *When Anger Hurts*, 106–9, 112–13.

6. McKay et al., *When Anger Hurts*, 95–96.

7. McKay et al., *When Anger Hurts*, 100.

8. McKay et al., *When Anger Hurts*, 102.

Notes

9. McKay et al., *When Anger Hurts*, 104–5.
10. Carol Tavris, *Anger: The Misunderstood Emotion*, rev. ed. (New York: Simon & Schuster, 1989), 42–46, 68–69, 128–60, Kindle.
11. Tavris, *Anger*, chap. 5. McKay et al., *When Anger Hurts*, 68–70.
12. McKay et al., *When Anger Hurts*, 70.
13. Cf. McKay et al., *When Anger Hurts*, 169.
14. Tavris, *Anger*, chap. 1.
15. McKay et al., *When Anger Hurts*, 170.
16. Tavris, *Anger*, chap. 2.
17. McKay et al., *When Anger Hurts*, 159–60.
18. McKay et al., *When Anger Hurts*, 151–54.
19. McKay et al., *When Anger Hurts*, 170–71.
20. McKay et al., *When Anger Hurts*, 184–89.
21. McKay et al., *When Anger Hurts*, 191.
22. McKay et al., *When Anger Hurts*, 226–32. Lerner points out that, for many women, assertiveness might require courage because self-assertion and separateness in an important relationship can provoke anxiety. Lerner, *The Dance of Anger*, 26.
23. Thich Nhat Hanh, *Anger: Wisdom for Cooling the Flames* (New York: Riverhead Books, 2001), 33–36.
24. McKay et al., *When Anger Hurts*, 245–49.
25. McKay et al., *When Anger Hurts*, 542–607.
26. Karmin, *Anger Management Workbook for Men*, 54–59.

CHAPTER 7

1. Matthew McKay and Patrick Fanning, *Self-Esteem: A Proven Program of Cognitive Techniques for Assessing, Improving, and Maintaining Your Self-Esteem*, 4th ed. (Oakland, CA: New Harbinger Publications, 2016), 55–56.
2. McKay and Fanning, *Self-Esteem*, 57–60.
3. Shirzad Chamine, *Positive Intelligence: Why Only 20% of Teams and Individuals Achieve Their True Potential and How You Can*

Achieve Yours (Austin, TX: Greenleaf Book Group Press, 2012), 87–91.

4. Chamine, *Positive Intelligence*, 95.

5. McKay and Fanning, *Self-Esteem*, 61.

6. McKay and Fanning, *Self-Esteem*, 69–78.

7. David L. Fleming, *The Spiritual Exercises of St. Ignatius: A Literal Translation and a Contemporary Reading* (St. Louis: The Institute of Jesuit Sources, 1978, 1991), 204–19.

8. Jules J. Toner, "Discernment in the Spiritual Exercises," in *A New Introduction to the Spiritual Exercises of St. Ignatius*, ed. J. Dister (Collegeville, MN: Liturgical Press, 1993), 64.

9. Timothy M. Gallagher, *The Discernment of Spirits: An Ignatian Guide for Everyday Living* (New York: Crossroad Publishing Company, 2005), chap. 1, Kindle. See also Mark E. Thibodeaux, SJ, *God's Voice Within: The Ignatian Way to Discover God's Will* (Chicago: Loyola Press, 2010), 12.

10. This list is an adaptation from McKay and Fanning, *Self-Esteem*, 144–59.

11. McKay and Fanning, *Self-Esteem*, 146.

12. McKay and Fanning, *Self-Esteem*, 146–47.

13. McKay and Fanning, *Self-Esteem*, 107–31.

14. David D. Burns, *Feeling Good: The New Mood Therapy* (New York: HarperCollins Publishers, 1980/1999), 73–74. McKay and Fanning, *Self-Esteem*, 149–50.

15. McKay and Fanning, *Self-Esteem*, 151–52.

16. McKay and Fanning, *Self-Esteem*, 77–78.

17. Burns, *Feeling Good*, 86.

18. McKay and Fanning, *Self-Esteem*, 79.

19. McKay and Fanning, *Self-Esteem*, 80.

20. McKay and Fanning, *Self-Esteem*, 109–29.

21. Burns, *Feeling Good*, 409.

22. McKay and Fanning, *Self-Esteem*, 107–40.

23. McKay and Fanning, *Self-Esteem*, 223–32.

Notes

CHAPTER 8

1. Phanxicô Xaviê Nguyễn Văn Thuận, *Năm Chiếc Bánh và Hai Con Cá*, 3rd ed. (Reichstett, France: Nhà Xuất Bản Định Hướng Tùng Thư, 1999), 13. This is my translation from the Vietnamese text. He was most likely referring to Bishop James E. Walsh, the Maryknoll bishop who was imprisoned for twelve years in China until his release in 1970.

2. *Alcoholics Anonymous Big Book*, 4th ed. (New York: Alcoholics Anonymous World Services, Inc., 2001), 158, Kindle.

3. Elisabeth Kübler-Ross and David Kessler, *Life Lessons: How Our Mortality Can Teach Us about Life and Living* (London: Simon & Schuster, 2000/2014), chap. 12, Kindle.

4. Elisabeth Kübler-Ross, *On Death and Dying: What the Dying Have to Teach Doctors, Nurses, Clergy and Their Own Families* (New York: Simon & Schuster, 1969/2014). Kindle.

5. Kübler-Ross, *On Death and Dying*, 124.

6. For an informed Catholic response to domestic violence against women, see United States Conference of Catholic Bishops, "When I Call for Help: A Pastoral Response to Domestic Violence against Women" (1992/2002), accessed May 1, 2024, https://www.usccb.org/topics/marriage-and-family-life-ministries/when-i-call-help-pastoral-response-domestic-violence.

7. In cases of domestic violence or abuse, the Catholic Church permits separation or civil divorce as a last resort to ensure the safety of women and children. See Canon Law #1153 and Catechism of the Catholic Church, #2383.

8. Eckhart Tolle, *The Power of Now: A Guide to Spiritual Enlightenment* (Vancouver, BC: Namaste Publishing and Novato, CA: New World Library, 1999/2004), 205, Kindle.

9. Tolle, *The Power of Now*, 82; Andrew Ryder, "The Sacrament of Now," *The Way* 46, no. 2 (April 2007): 7–18. I am indebted to Ryder's article for providing valuable insights.

THE BREATH OF CHRIST

10. The late cardinal secretly wrote *The Road of Hope* while in detention and had it published with the help of local Catholics. He also shared the good news with others while in prison, including the prison guards, and attracted many to the Catholic faith.

11. Tolle, *The Power of Now*, 187.

12. "IASP Announces Revised Definition of Pain," published July 16, 2020, https://www.iasp-pain.org/PublicationsNews/News Detail.aspx?ItemNumber=10475.

13. Michael Brady made a similar point when he wrote, "Suffering: a subject suffers when and only when she has an unpleasant or negative affective experience that she minds, where to mind some state is to have an occurrent desire that it not be occurring." Michael S. Brady, *Suffering and Virtue* (Oxford: Oxford University Press, 2018), 27, Kindle.

14. Tolle, *The Power of Now*, 187.

15. Tolle, *The Power of Now*, 84.

16. Jean-Pierre De Caussade, *Abandonment to Divine Providence: With Letters of Father de Caussade on the Practice of Self-Abandonment*, trans. E. J. Strickland, ed. J. Ramière (San Francisco: Ignatius Press, 2011), 29, Kindle.

17. De Caussade, *Abandonment to Divine Providence*, 7.

CHAPTER 9

1. St. Augustine, *The City of God*, trans. Marcus Dods, intro. Thomas Merton (New York: The Modern Library, 2000), 17.

2. Eckhart Tolle, *The Power of Now: A Guide to Spiritual Enlightenment* (Vancouver, BC: Namaste Publishing and Novato, CA: New World Library, 1999/2004), 22–23.

3. Tolle, *The Power of Now*, 45–48.

Notes

COMING HOME

1. Elisabeth Kübler-Ross and David Kessler, *Life Lessons: How Our Mortality Can Teach Us about Life and Living* (London: Simon & Schuster, 2000, 2014), chap. 8.

www.ingramcontent.com/pod-product-compliance
Lightning Source LLC
Chambersburg PA
CBHW070555160426
43199CB00014B/2512